English Graphics Grow-up
Grammar

한번 보면 바로 생각나는
★ ★ ★
영문법

JN360698

한번 보면 바로 생각나는
★ ★ ★
영문법

발 행	2020년 2월 5일
발행인	이재명
발행처	삼지사
등록번호	제406-2011-000021호
주 소	경기도 파주시 산남로 47-10
Tel	031)948-4502, 948-4564
Fax	031)948-4508
ISBN	978-89-7358-433-8 (13740)

책값은 뒤표지에 있습니다.
이 교재의 내용을 사전 허가없이 전재하거나 복제할 경우 법적인
제재를 받게 됨을 알려드립니다.
잘못된 책은 구입하신 서점에서 교환해 드립니다.

English Graphics Grow-up
Grammar

한번 보면 바로 생각나는

영문법

Free MP3 다운로드
www.samjisa.com

SAMJI BOOKS

한번보면 바로 생각나는
영문법은?

영문법은 외우는 게 아닙니다.
시험 볼 것이 아니라면 그저 쑥 훑어보면 족합니다. 그러나 그렇다고 한번 보고 집어 던지라는 것이 아닙니다. 문법은 우리가 늘 접하는 것입니다.
한번 머리에 담아두고 무언가 비슷한 것이 잡히면 한 번 들춰보고 확인하고, 헷갈릴 때도 잠깐 열어서 확인해보는 것이 문법책을 제대로 사용하는 방법입니다

EGG는 마치 계란을 깨뜨릴 때처럼 여러분의 영문법에 대한 껍질을 깨주는 책입니다.

이 책의 구성

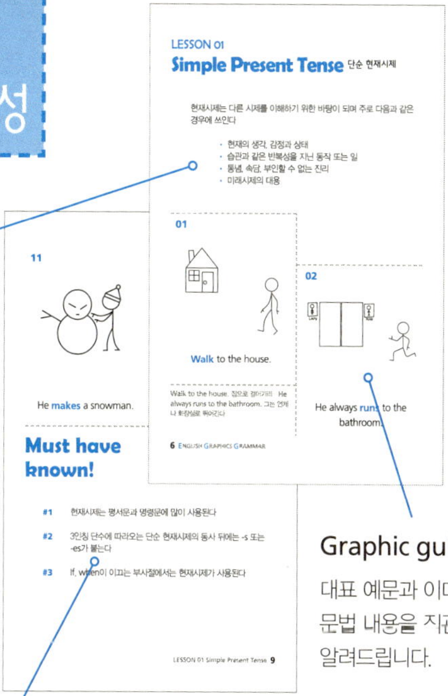

핵심 요약

해당 문법의 가장 핵심적인 내용을 정리했습니다.

Graphic guide

대표 예문과 이미지로 문법 내용을 직관적으로 알려드립니다.

Must have known

해당 문법의 유용한 팁과 확장 활용에 대한 정보를 정리했습니다.

EXERCISE ACTIVITY

10 레슨마다 중간 점검할 수 있는 퀴즈를 수록했습니다.

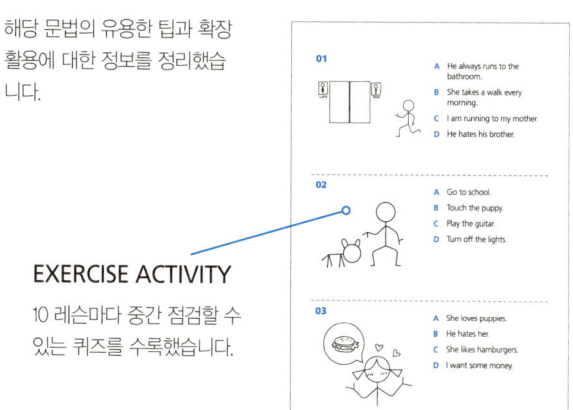

순서

LESSON 01	Simple Present Tense 단순 현재시제	p.8
LESSON 02	Object Pronouns 목적격 대명사	p.12
LESSON 03	Subject Pronouns 주격 대명사	p.16
LESSON 04	Key Word 핵심어	p.20
LESSON 05	Possessive Pronouns (Adjectives) 소유격 대명사	p.24
LESSON 06	Demonstratives 지시형용사	p.28
LESSON 07	Simple Past Tense 단순 과거시제	p.32
LESSON 08	Present Continuous 현재진행	p.36
LESSON 09	Adjectives 형용사	p.40
LESSON 10	Articles 관사	p.44
	EXCERCISE ACTIVITY	p.48
LESSON 11	Past tense of Be be동사의 과거시제	p.60
LESSON 12	Past Continuous 과거진행	p.64
LESSON 13	HAVE – Present and Past Tenses Have 동사의 현재형과 과거형	p.68
LESSON 14	Possessive Case and "OF" Expressions 소유를 나타내는 표현들	p.72
LESSON 15	Wh - Questions wh – 의문문	p.76
LESSON 16	A lot of / a few 수량형용사	p.80
LESSON 17	Singular and Plural Nouns 단수와 복수	p.84
LESSON 18	Future – To be going to 미래를 나타내는 begoing to	p.88
LESSON 19	Future – Will 미래	p.92
LESSON 20	Adjectives – Comparison 형용사의 비교급	p.96
	EXCERCISE ACTIVITY	p.100
LESSON 21	Tag Questions 부가 의문문	p.112
LESSON 22	Interrogative Verb Forms 동사 의문형	p.116
LESSON 23	Adverbs 부사	p.120
LESSON 24	Conjunctions 접속사	p.124
LESSON 25	Expletives 허사	p.128

LESSON 26	Prepositions of Time 시간을 나타내는 전치사	p.132
LESSON 27	Prepositions of Place 장소를 나타내는 전치사	p.136
LESSON 28	Abstract Nouns 추상명사	p.140
LESSON 29	Present Perfect 현재완료	p.144
LESSON 30	Past Perfect 과거완료	p.148
	EXCERCISE ACTIVITY	p.152
LESSON 31	Active / Passive Voice 능동태와 수동태	p.164
LESSON 32	Adjective Clause 형용사구	p.168
LESSON 33	Too much / Too many 양이 많은 / 수가 많은	p.172
LESSON 34	Future Perfect Progressive 미래완료진행	p.176
LESSON 35	Present Perfect Progressive 현재완료진행	p.180
LESSON 36	Past Perfect Progressive 과거완료진행	p.184
LESSON 37	Future Perfect 미래완료	p.188
LESSON 38	Adverbs of Frequency 빈도부사	p.192
LESSON 39	Reflexive Pronouns 재귀대명사	p.196
LESSON 40	For / Since 시간을 나타내는 전치사	p.200
	EXCERCISE ACTIVITY	p.204
LESSON 41	Other / Another 부정대명사 the other과 another	p.216
LESSON 42	Adverbs of Time 시간을 나타내는 부사	p.220
LESSON 43	Comparison of Adverbs 부사의 비교급	p.224
LESSON 44	Body Parts 신체부위	p.228
LESSON 45	Count / Non-Count Nouns 셀 수 있는 명사와, 셀 수 없는 명사	p.232
LESSON 46	Contractions 축약형	p.236
LESSON 47	Clock Time 시계읽기	p.240
LESSON 48	Do / Does / Did do 동사	p.244
LESSON 49	Adverb Clauses 부사구	p.248
LESSON 50	Noun Clause 명사절	p.252
	EXCERCISE ACTIVITY	p.256

LESSON 01
Simple Present Tense 단순 현재시제

현재시제는 다른 시제를 이해하기 위한 바탕이 되며 주로 다음과 같은 경우에 쓰인다.

- 현재의 생각, 감정과 상태
- 습관과 같은 반복성을 지닌 동작 또는 일
- 통념, 속담, 부인할 수 없는 진리
- 미래시제의 대용

01

Walk to the house.

Walk to the house. 집으로 걸어가라   He always runs to the bathroom. 그는 언제나 화장실로 뛰어간다

02

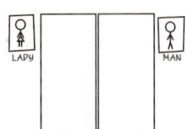

He always **runs** to the bathroom.

03

Look at the sky.

Look at the sky. 하늘을 봐   Touch the puppy. 강아지를 만져라

04

Touch the puppy.

05

She **knows** everything about me.

She knows everything about me. 그녀는 나에 관해 모든 것을 알고 있다   Push the button. 버튼을 눌러라

06

Push the button.

LESSON 01 Simple Present Tense

07

He usually **sleeps** at school.

He usually sleeps at school. 그는 보통 학교에서 잔다   She likes hamburgers. 그녀는 햄버거를 좋아한다

08

She **likes** hamburgers.

09

Visit a hospital.

Visit a hospital. 병원을 방문해라   She speaks Korean. 그녀는 한국말을 한다

10

She **speaks** Korean.

11

He **makes** a snowman.

Must have known!

He makes a snowman. 그는 눈사람을 만든다 Throw the ball. 공을 던져라

12

Throw the ball.

#1   현재시제는 평서문과 명령문에 많이 사용된다.

#2   3인칭 단수에 따라오는 단순 현재시제의 동사 뒤에는 -s 또는 -es가 붙는다.

#3   If, when이 이끄는 부사절에서는 현재시제가 사용된다.

LESSON 01 Simple Present Tense   **11**

LESSON 02
Object Pronouns 목적격 대명사

목적어는 문장에서 동사나 전치사의 표적이 되는 성분이다.
대명사란 명사를 '대리'해 주는 역할을 하고, 주격, 목적격, 소유격이 있다.
따라서 목적격 대명사는 목적어의 자리에 쓰인 대명사를 의미하며
'~(를)을.'로 해석할 수 있다.

목적격 대명사는 다음과 같다.
   me   us   you   him   her   it   them

01

Give a pencil to **her**.

Give a pencil to her. 그녀에게 연필을 줘
Tell him to give us money. 우리에게 돈을
주라고 그에게 말해

02

Tell **him** to give us money.

03

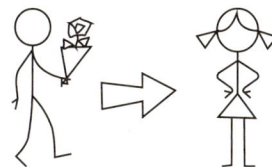

Walk to **her** and give **her** a rose.

05

She needs **him** to park her car.

She needs him to park her car. 그녀는 주차를 하기 위해 그가 필요하다   He would like her to clean his room. 그는 그녀가 그의 방을 청소했으면 한다

Walk to her and give her a rose. 그녀에게 걸어가 그녀에게 장미를 줘   She wants him to stop running. 그녀는 그가 그만 뛰길 바란다

04

She wants **him** to stop running.

06

He would like **her** to clean his room.

LESSON 02 Object Pronouns

07

He gives many presents to **her**.

08

He loves **her** very much.

09

Go with **them** to mars.

10

Run to **him** and catch him with a net.

He gives many presents to her. 그는 그녀에게 많은 선물을 준다   He loves her very much. 그는 그녀를 매우 사랑한다

Go with them to mars. 그들과 함께 화성에 가라   Run to him and catch him with a net. 그에게 달려가서 그물로 그를 잡아라

11

Put **it** in his pocket.

Must have known!

Put it in his pocket. 그의 주머니에 그것을 넣어라   She wants them to get out of the house. 그녀는 집에서 그들이 나가길 바란다

12

She wants **them** to get out of the house.

#1   전치사 다음에는 목적격을 사용한다.

#2   문법적인 격이란 다른 낱말과 관계상의 지위라고 할 수 있다.

#3   목적격 대명사는 간접,직접 목적어의 형태로 모두 쓰일 수 있다.

LESSON 03
Subject Pronouns 주격 대명사

주격 대명사는 문장에서 주어로 쓰이는 대명사를 가리키며
'~(은, 는, 이)가'로 해석된다.

주격 대명사의 종류는 다음과 같다.
  I   we   you   he   she   it   they

01

He is an artist.

He is an artist. 그는 예술가이다   They are going to mars. 그들은 화성으로 가고 있다

02

They are going to mars.

03

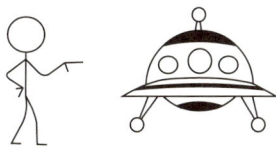

It is a spaceship.

04

He is writing on the board.

05

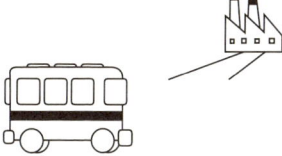

We are going on a field trip.

06

They are his parents.

It is a spaceship. 그것은 우주선이다 He is writing on the board. 그가 칠판에 적고 있다

We are going on a field trip. 우리는 견학을 가는 중이다 They are his parents. 그들은 그의 부모님이다

LESSON 03 Subject Pronouns **17**

07

Wave to him if **you** know him.

09

He thinks he can fly.

He thinks he can fly. 그는 날 수 있다고 생각한다   She looked sad. 그녀는 슬퍼 보였다

Wave to him if you know him. 네가 그를 알면 손을 흔들어라   Eat it if it is not too hot. 너무 뜨겁지 않으면 먹어라

08

Eat it if **it** is not too hot.

10

She looked sad.

18 ENGLISH GRAPHICS GRAMMAR

11

He has destroyed her snowman.

Must have known!

He has destroyed her snowman. 그가 그녀의 눈사람을 망쳤다   He fell down. 그는 넘어졌다

12

He fell down.

#1 구어체에서는 주격 대명사의 자리를 목적격 대명사가 차지하기도 한다.

#2 they는 he, she, it의 복수이기 때문에, 꼭 사람만을 가리키지는 않는다.

#3 주격대명사는 앞의 명사를 반복하는 것을 피할 때 사용된다.

LESSON 04
Key Word 핵심어

Key Word는 품사와 위치를 불문하고 의미 전달 및 해석에 있어서 핵심이 되는 존재이다.

01

Thank God It is **Friday**.

Thank God It is Friday. 기다리던 금요일이 왔다 The color of a lobster is red. 바닷 가재 색깔은 빨간색 이다

02

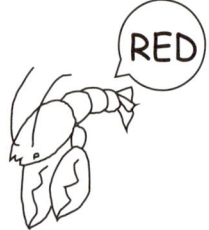

The color of a lobster is **red**.

03

Christmas comes
on a **Thursday** this year.

Christmas comes on a Thursday this year. 이번 년의 크리스마스는 목요일이다
One plus one is two. 1더하기 1은 2이다

04

$$1 + 1 = 2$$

One plus **one** is **two**.

05

A dog has **four** paws.

A dog has four paws. 개는 발이 4개이다
January is the first month of the year.
1월은 한 해의 첫째 달이다

06

January is the **first** month
of the year.

LESSON 04 Key Word

07

She has **blue** eyes.

08

October second is my birthday.

09

Take bus number **1000** to go to Seoul.

10

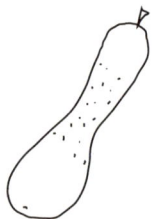

A cucumber is **green**.

She has blue eyes. 그녀는 파란 눈을 가지고 있다   October second is my birthday. 10월 2일은 내 생일이다

Take bus number 1000 to go to Seoul. 서울에 가기 위해 1000번 버스를 타라
A cucumber is green. 오이는 초록색 이다

11

He hates to go to work on **Monday**.

Must have known!

He hates to go to work on Monday. 그는 월요일에 일하러 가기 싫어한다   His height when he sits is 90cm. 그의 앉은키는 90cm 이다

12

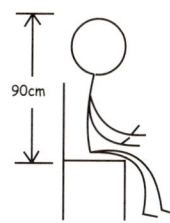

His height when he sits is **90**cm.

#1   Key Word는 대체로 명사나 형용사의 형태로 쓰인다.

LESSON 05
Possessive Pronouns (Adjectives)
소유격 대명사

명사의 주인을 가리킬 때 사용되는 대명사를 소유격 대명사라고 부른다 '~의'로 해석된다.

소유격의 종류는 다음과 같다.
    my   our   your   his   her   its   their

01

Don't touch **my** money!

02

Those are **our** seats.

Don't touch my money! 내 돈을 만지지 마!
Those are our seats. 거기는 우리 자리들이다

03

She asked me for **my** phone number.

05

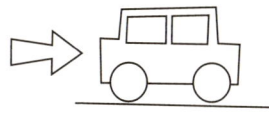

That's **his** car.

That's his car. 저건 그의 자동차이다   My friends bring their gifts to my house. 나의 친구들이 집으로 선물을 가지고 온다

She asked me for my phone number. 그녀는 나의 전화번호를 물었다   The boy likes his banana. 소년은 그의 바나나를 좋아한다

04

The boy likes **his** banana.

06

My friends bring **their** gifts to **my** house.

LESSON 05 Possessive Pronouns(Adjectives)

07

The boy likes **his** big teddy bear.

09

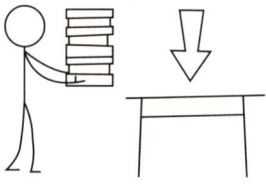

Put **your** books on the desk.

Put your books on the desk. 너의 책들을 책상 위에 올려놓아라   That's her handbag. 저건 그녀의 핸드백이다

The boy likes his big teddy bear. 소년은 그의 큰 곰 인형을 좋아한다   We are bringing our notebooks to class. 우리는 노트를 가지고 학교에 간다

08

We are bringing **our** notebooks to class.

10

That's **her** handbag.

11

Korea is **our** country.

Must have known!

Korea is our country. 한국은 우리나라다
She threw her papers on his desk. 그녀
는 종이들을 그의 책상 위에 던졌다

12

She threw **her** papers on **his** desk.

#1   its & it's : its는 it의 소유격이고, it's는 it is의 축약형이다.

#2   소유격 대명사 다음에는 반드시 명사를 두어야 한다.

#3   소유격 대명사 + 명사의 조합 대신 mine, ours, yours, his, hers, theirs의 소유대명사(소유'격' 대명사와는 다름!)를 쓸 수도 있다.

LESSON 06
Demonstratives 지시형용사

지시형용사는 명사를 이것, 저것으로 가리키며 꾸며 주는 형용사이다.

This와 these는 가까이 있는 명사를 꾸밀 때,
That과 those는 멀리 있는 명사를 꾸밀 때 사용된다.

01

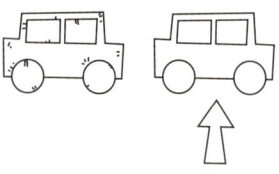

This car looks cleaner **than** that one.

This car looks cleaner than that one.
이 차가 저 차보다 깨끗해 보인다 Those people are students. 그 사람들은 학생들이다

02

Those people are students.

03

These bags are really heavy.

05

She will mail **this** letter.

She will mail this letter. 그녀가 이 편지를 보낼 것이다   That little girl is pretty. 저 여자아이는 예쁘다

These bags are really heavy. 이 가방들은 정말 무겁다   Those English books are really good. 그 영어 책들은 정말 좋다

04

Those English books are really good.

06

That little girl is pretty.

LESSON 06 Demonstratives **29**

07

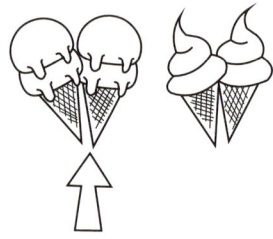

These ice creams are better than **those** are.

These ice creams are better than those are. 이 아이스크림들이 저 아이스크림들보다 낫다   This shirt is too big for him. 이 셔츠는 그에게 너무 크다

08

This shirt is too big for him.

09

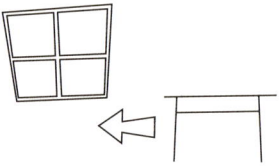

Push **that** desk to the window.

Push that desk to the window. 그 책상을 창가로 밀어라   Put this money in the bank. 이 돈을 은행에 넣어라

10

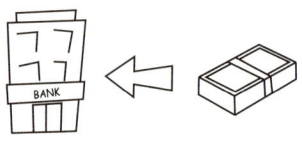

Put **this** money in the bank.

11

That candy is mine!

Must have known!

That candy is mine! 그 사탕은 내 거야!
Pick that trash up around you. 네 주위의 그 쓰레기들을 주워라

12

Pick that trash up around you.

#1   단수 명사는 this / that으로, 복수 명사는 these / those로 꾸며 준다.

#2   these는 this의 복수 형태로, those는 that의 복수 형태로 사용된다.

#3   This와 these는 that과 those에 비해 심리적으로 더 '가까운 것'을 의미한다.

#4   지시형용사와는 달리 뒤에 명사 없이 쓰는 지시대명사는 사물에만 쓴다.

LESSON 07
Simple Past Tense 단순 과거시제

과거시제는 다음과 같은 상황에 쓰인다.

- 과거에 있었던 일
- 역사적 사실
- 과거의 습관

주로 과거를 나타내는 부사와 함께 쓴다.

01

He **walked** to work today.

He walked to work today. 그는 오늘 직장에 걸어갔다 The girl jumped on the chair. 소녀가 의자 위로 뛰었다

02

The girl **jumped** on the chair.

03

Closed door

04

A boy **drew** a house on the street.

05

He **parked** his car in the garage.

06

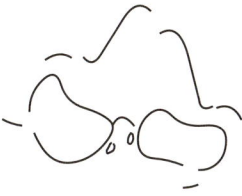

Smashed glasses

Closed door 닫힌 문   A boy drew a house on the street. 소년이 길에 집을 그렸다

He parked his car in the garage. 그는 차고 안에 차를 주차했다   Smashed glasses 산산조각난 안경.

07

The UFO **flew** upward.

09

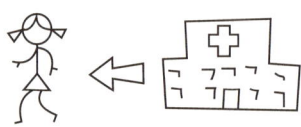

She **went** out from the hospital.

She went out from the hospital. 그녀는 병원에서 나왔다   A boy ate too much. 소년은 너무 많이 먹었다

The UFO flew upward. UFO가 위로 날아올랐다   I wrote my name in Spanish. 난 내 이름을 스페인어로 적었다

08

I **wrote** my name in Spanish.

10

A boy **ate** too much.

11

The dog **drank** all of my coke.

Must have known!

The dog drank all of my coke. 개가 내 콜라를 다 마셨다   Snow White built a white castle. 백설공주는 하얀 성을 지었다

12

Snow White **built** a white castle.

#1   규칙 동사의 과거형은 단어의 끝에 –ed를 붙이지만, 불규칙 동사는 과거형이 제각기 다르다.

#2   After, before 등 때를 명확히 알려주는 부사와 함께 과거완료 대신에 쓰일 수 있다.

#3   과거시제의 동사형태는 명사 앞에 붙어 형용사로 쓰이기도 한다.

LESSON 08
Present Continuous 현재진행

현재진행형은 지금 바로 이순간 진행되고 있는 동작을 표현할 때 쓴다.

'~하는 중이다'로 해석할 수 있다.

01

A thief **is running** away from a policeman.

A thief is running away from a policeman. 도둑이 경찰에게서 도망치고 있다
A boy is eating a whole pizza. 소년이 피자를 다 먹어치우고 있다.

02

A boy **is eating** a whole pizza.

36 ENGLISH GRAPHICS GRAMMAR

03

The dog **is drinking** all of my coke.

04

A baby **is watching** TV.

05

She **is talking** with a teacher.

06

A fairy **is taking** a bath in the pond.

The dog is drinking all of my coke. 개가 내 콜라를 다 마시고 있다   A baby is watching TV. 아기가 TV를 보고 있다

She is talking with a teacher. 그녀가 선생님과 말하고 있다   A fairy is taking a bath in the pond. 선녀가 연못에서 목욕을 하고 있다

07

A lady **is wearing** earrings.

A lady is wearing earrings. 여자가 귀고리를 하고 있다   A guy is sleeping on the chair. 남자가 의자에서 자고 있다

08

A guy **is sleeping** on the chair.

09

A person **is washing** his (her) hands.

A person is washing his (her) hands. 한 사람이 손을 씻고 있다   A guy is hiding under the desk. 남자가 책상 아래 숨어 있다

10

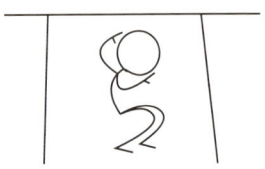

A guy **is hiding** under the desk.

38 ENGLISH GRAPHICS GRAMMAR

11

A boy **is falling** down the stairs.

Must have known!

A boy is falling down the stairs. 소년이 계단에서 굴러떨어지고 있다   A dog is trying to catch a cat. 개가 고양이를 잡으려 하고 있다

12

A dog **is trying** to catch a cat.

#1   am / is / are + 동사 -ing

#2   소유, 감정, 인지 등을 나타내는 상태동사는 진행형으로 쓰지 않는다.

#3   현재진행형이 미래를 나타내는 부사와 함께 쓰이면 가까운 미래를 나타낸다.

#4   Always, constantly 등의 부사와 함께 쓰이면 동작의 반복, 행위자의 습관을 나타낸다.

LESSON 09
Adjectives 형용사

형용사는 명사를 꾸며 주는 품사이다.

사물의 모양, 수량, 성질 등을 나타낸다.

01

He's **strong**.

He's strong. 그는 강하다   That man is old. 저 남자는 늙었다

02

That man is **old**.

03

The king has **big** ears.

05

The woman in the **black** hat.

The woman in the black hat. 검은 모자를 쓴 여자 My glass is empty. 내 컵이 비어 있다

The king has big ears. 왕은 큰 귀를 가지고 있다 The giraffe has a long neck. 기린은 긴 목을 가지고 있다

04

The giraffe has a **long** neck.

06

My glass is **empty**.

07

The Eiffel tower is **high**.

08

The horse runs **fast**.

09

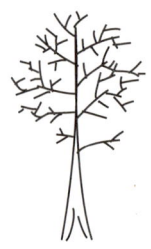

The tree has **many** twigs.

10

The turtle is too **slow**.

The Eiffel tower is high. 에펠 탑은 높다
The horse runs fast. 말은 빨리 달린다

The tree has many twigs. 그 나무에는 잔가지들이 많다 The turtle is too slow. 거북은 너무 느리다

11

These boxes are **heavy**.

Must have known!

These boxes are heavy. 이 상자들은 무겁다
That man is thin. 저 남자는 홀쭉하다

12

That man is **thin**.

#1   형용사 + 명사 또는 be동사 / 감각동사 + 형용사

#2   형용사의 어순 : 크기 + 모양 + 나이 + 성질 및 상태

#3   the + 형용사는 명사로 쓰인다.

#4   한 명사를 여러 형용사가 꾸밀때에는 관사 / 지시형용사 / 대명사의 소유격 + 수량형용사 + 일반형용사 순으로 쓰인다.

LESSON 10
Articles 관사

관사는 형용사의 일종으로 그 뒤에 오는 명사가 특정한 것인지,
일반적인 것인지를 가르쳐 준다.

부정관사인 a, an과 정관사 the로 나뉜다.
부정관사 a / an은 '하나'라는 뜻을 가지고 있다.
정관사 the는 서로 이미 알고 있는 명사를 가리킬 때 쓰며
우리말의 '그'에 해당한다.

01

The top of **the** mountain

The top of the mountain 산꼭대기   He is an Indian. 그는 인도 사람이다

02

He is **an** Indian.

03

He is **a** student.

04

He is a student. 그는 학생이다 A guy is sleeping on the bed. 남자가 침대 위에서 자고 있다

A guy is sleeping on **the** bed.

05

There is **a** computer and **a** puppy on the desk.

There is a computer and a puppy on the desk. 책상 위에 컴퓨터와 강아지가 있다
The boy is holding an ice-cream. 소년이 아이스크림을 들고 있다

06

The boy is holding **an** icecream.

LESSON 10 Articles **45**

07

She has **a** fancy sports car.

08

An ice cube is in **the** cup.

She has a fancy sports car. 그녀는 최고급 스포츠카를 가지고 있다   An ice cube is in the cup. 각얼음이 컵 안에 있다

09

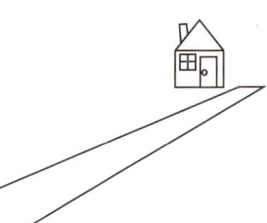

The house at the very end of **the** street

10

The girl is drinking **the** coke with **a** straw.

The house at the very end of the street 거리 제일 끝에 있는 집   The girl is drinking the coke with a straw. 여자아이가 빨대로 콜라를 마시고 있다

11

Snow White ate
a poisoned apple.

Must have known!

Snow White ate a poisoned apple. 백설공주가 독 사과를 먹었다 Pinocchio is made of wood. 피노키오는 나무로 만들어졌다

12

Pinocchio is made of wood.

#1 발음이 a, e, i, o, u로 시작되는 단어 앞에는 an을 쓴다.

#2 부정관사는 셀 수 있는 명사의 단수형에만 붙인다.

#3 병, 계절, 식사시간, 운동 등 앞에서는 관사 a / an을 붙이지 않는다.

#4 고유명사가 인공물일때, by 교통수단 으로 쓰일때 정관사 the를 붙이지 않는다.

다음 이미지를 보고 우측에서 적절한 답에 표시하세요.

01

- A He always runs to the bathroom.
- B She takes a walk every morning.
- C I am running to my mother.
- D He hates his brother.

02

- A Go to school.
- B Touch the puppy.
- C Play the guitar.
- D Turn off the lights.

03

- A She loves puppies.
- B He hates her.
- C She likes hamburgers.
- D I want some money.

04

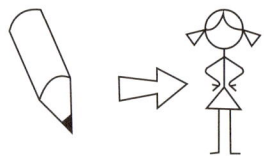

- **A** Go to hospital.
- **B** Shut the door.
- **C** Pass me the salt.
- **D** Give a pencil to her.

05

- **A** I want you to get away from me.
- **B** She needs him to park her car.
- **C** She eats sandwich every morning.
- **D** He has a stomachache.

06

- **A** Go with them to Mars.
- **B** Take care of the baby.
- **C** Open the door.
- **D** Give me some crayons.

07

A She is my sister.
B He is a movie star.
C We are friends.
D He is an artist.

08

A It is a piano.
B It is a spaceship.
C It is an apple.
D It is a bicycle.

09

A He has destroyed her snowman.
B He gives her a bunch of flowers.
C We are playing basketball.
D She is throwing a snowball to him.

10

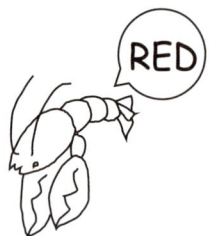

A She likes to eat shrimps.
B Lobsters live in oceans.
C The color of a lobster is red.
D A duck has two legs.

11

A Three plus four is seven.
B One plus one is two.
C Five minus four is one.
D Six minus one is five.

$1 + 1 = 2$

12

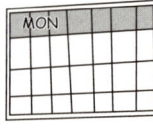

A He hates to go to work on Monday.
B I am having a lunch with my sister.
C He will come back home on Thursday.
D She gives him a birthday present.

13

A He goes to library.
B The boy likes his banana.
C She is listening to music.
D The girl is hungry.

14

A I was absent yesterday.
B He is playing soccer.
C She is going to church.
D We are bringing our notebooks to class.

15

A I have been to France.
B She lives in Canada.
C Korea is our country.
D He is going to the airport.

16

A These bags are really heavy.
B Watermelons have seeds.
C The clothes are dirty.
D The bicycle has two wheels.

17

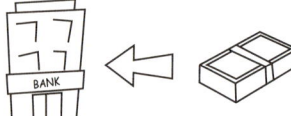

A Let's go to the gym.
B Put this money in the bank.
C Come back here right now.
D Don't steal my money.

18

A He ate my chocolate.
B Where is my wallet?
C I want to drink a coke.
D That candy is mine!

19

- **A** He walked to work today.
- **B** She studies hard.
- **C** Let's take a bus.
- **D** We stayed here for 2 hours.

20

- **A** Blue pencil
- **B** Hard rock
- **C** Smashed glasses
- **D** Hot water

21

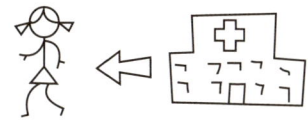

- **A** She is a high school student.
- **B** She went out from the hospital.
- **C** We graduated from the same school.
- **D** I have a toothache.

22

A I love to eat spaghettis.

B She likes to play computer games.

C A boy is eating a whole pizza.

D I am brushing my teeth.

23

A A baby is watching TV.

B We are taking a walk.

C She is writing a letter.

D He is driving his car.

24

A A boy is wearing glasses.

B A baby is eating a cookie.

C A lady is wearing earrings.

D A girl is drinking a cup of milk.

25

- A He's strong.
- B She's skinny.
- C He's weak.
- D She's chubby.

26

- A I am hungry.
- B The water is cold.
- C My glass is empty.
- D The sky is sunny.

27

- A The rabbit has long ears.
- B The turtle is too slow.
- C The giraffe has a long neck.
- D The crocodile has a big mouth.

28

A A boy is swimming in the sea.
B A girl is playing a piano.
C A guy is sleeping on the bed.
D A lady is reading a newspaper.

29

A An ice cube is in the cup.
B A coin is in the pocket.
C An eraser is in the pencil case.
D A carrot is in the refrigerator.

30

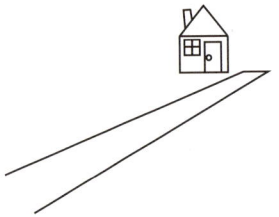

A The big tree next to the house
B The house at the very end of the street
C The hospital in front of the school
D The dog across the street

EXERCISE ACTIVITY ANSWERS

01	A	16	A
02	B	17	B
03	C	18	D
04	D	19	A
05	B	20	C
06	A	21	B
07	D	22	C
08	B	23	A
09	A	24	C
10	C	25	A
11	B	26	C
12	A	27	B
13	B	28	C
14	D	29	A
15	C	30	B

나의 정답 개수

/30

정답 개수가 **24**개 이상이라면
➔ 이제 다음 레슨을 공부하세요

정답 개수가 **24**개 이하라면
➔ 레슨 1로 돌아가서 복습하세요

LESSON 11
Past tense of Be be동사의 과거시제

be동사는 '~이다'와 '있다'의 뜻을 가진 기본적인 동사이다.

주어의 인칭과 수, 시제에 따라 각각 다른 형태로 쓰인다.
단수의 경우 was, 복수의 경우 were로 쓴다.

01

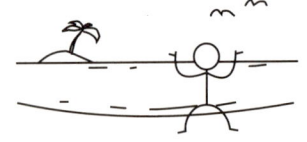

I **was** at the beach yesterday.

I was at the beach yesterday. 난 어제 해변에 있었어   His eyes were big from tears. 그의 눈에는 눈물이 가득했다

02

His eyes **were** big from tears.

03

The girl **was** a student.

05

The boy **was** in the box.

The boy was in the box. 소년은 박스 안에 있었다   It was sunny yesterday. 어제는 맑았다

The girl was a student. 소녀는 학생이었다
The men were outside of the house.
남자들은 집 밖에 있었다

04

The men **were** outside of the house.

06

It **was** sunny yesterday.

LESSON 11 Past tense of Be

07

We **were** at the bus stop.

09

The beast **was** really hungry during lunchtime.

The beast was really hungry during lunchtime. 야수는 점심시간에 매우 배고팠다
They were late for the bus. 그들은 버스 시간에 늦었다

We were at the bus stop. 우리는 버스 정류장에 있었다   She was a teacher last year. 작년에 그녀는 선생님이었다

08

She **was** a teacher last year.

10

They **were** late for the bus.

11

The king **was** a beggar
when he was young.

Must have known!

The king was a beggar when he was young. 왕은 어렸을 때 거지였다   The beast was a handsome man. 야수는 멋진 남자였다

12

The beast **was**
a handsome man.

#1   부정문을 만들때에는 be 동사 뒤에 not을 붙인다.

#2   1인칭 & 3인칭인 겨우 was, 2인칭인 경우엔 were을 쓴다.

#3   '～이 있다' 라는 의미로 쓰일땐 장소나 때를 나타내는 부사나 구와 함께 쓰인다.

LESSON 11 Past tense of Be

LESSON 12
Past Continuous 과거진행

과거진행형은 과거의 한 시점에서 진행 중인 동작을 나타낸다.

'…하고 있는 중이었다'로 해석한다.

01

She **was skating** at the square.

She was skating at the square. 그녀는 광장에서 스케이트를 타고 있었다 A fire was blazing in the frying pan. 프라이팬 위에서 불이 타오르고 있었다

02

A fire **was blazing** in the frying pan.

03

They **were carrying** boxes.

04

The dog **was jumping** on the ground.

05

The policeman **was eating** a doughnut.

The policeman was eating a doughnut. 경찰관이 도넛을 먹고 있었다 Santa Claus was having trouble with the reindeer. 산타클로스는 사슴과 말썽을 겪고 있었다

They were carrying boxes. 그들은 박스를 나르고 있었다 The dog was jumping on the ground. 개가 땅 위에서 뛰고 있었다

06

Santa Claus **was having** trouble with the reindeer.

07

The students **were lying** on the field.

08

He **was taking** a bath in the pond.

09

The girl **was drinking** a cup of coffee.

10

The people **were singing**.

The students were lying on the field. 학생들이 운동장에 누워 있었다 He was taking a bath in the pond. 그는 연못에서 목욕을 하고 있었다

The girl was drinking a cup of coffee. 여자아이가 커피를 마시고 있었다 The people were singing. 사람들이 노래를 부르고 있었다

11

The boy **was cooking** ramen.

Must have known!

The boy was cooking ramen. 그 소년은 라면을 끓이고 있었다   They were sleeping on the couch. 그들은 소파에서 자고 있었다

12

They **were sleeping** on the couch.

#1 Was / were + 동사 -ing

#2 과거진행형은 특정시간에 일어나고 있던 일을 나타낸다.

#3 동시에 둘 이상의 일이 나타났을 경우엔 단순과거형과 함께 쓰이기도 한다.

LESSON 13
HAVE – Present and Past Tenses
Have 동사의 현재형과 과거형

have 동사는 be동사와 같이 중요한 기능을 가지는 기본 동사이다. 크게 '가지다, 먹다, 시키다'의 뜻을 가진다.

눈에 보이는 물건뿐만이 아닌 추상적인 대상에도 사용 가능하다. 다른 동사와 결합하여 시제를 나타내는 조동사로도 쓰인다.

01

The girl **has** a frying pan.

The girl has a frying pan. 소녀는 프라이팬을 가지고 있다   The boy has a scar on his hand. 소년은 손에 흉터가 있다

02

The boy **has** a scar on his hand.

03

We **have** a stadium in our school.

05

They **have** many dogs in the vacant lot.

They have many dogs in the vacant lot. 그들은 공터에 많은 개들을 가지고 있다   He has a toothache. 그는 치통이 있다

We have a stadium in our school. 우리 학교에는 경기장이 있다   The woman has a diamond ring. 여자는 다이아 반지를 가지고 있다

04

The woman **has** a diamond ring.

06

He **has** a toothache.

LESSON 13 HAVE – Present and Past Tenses

07

The woman **has** five children.

09

The girl **had** cake and coffee for dessert.

The girl had cake and coffee for dessert.
소녀는 후식으로 커피와 케이크를 먹었다
Pinocchio has wooden hands. 피노키오는
나무로 된 손을 가지고 있다

The woman has five children. 여자는
다섯 명의 자식이 있다   He vomited
everything he had eaten. 그는 먹은 것을
다 토해 버렸다

08

He vomited everything he **had** eaten.

10

Pinocchio **has** wooden hands.

11

Hellboy **has** a broken horn on his head.

Must have known!

Hellboy has a broken horn on his head. 헬보이는 머리에 깨진 뿔을 가지고 있다 Cats have sharp claws. 고양이들은 날카로운 발톱을 가지고 있다

12

Cats **have** sharp claws.

#1 주어가 3인칭 단수일 경우 have가 아닌 has로 쓴다.

#2 과거시제는 주어에 상관없이 had로 쓴다.

#3 사역동사로 쓰인 have는 have + 목적어 + 과거분사 / to v의 형태로 쓴다.

LESSON 13 HAVE – Present and Past Tenses

LESSON 14
Possessive Case and "OF" Expressions 소유를 나타내는 표현들

소유를 나타내는 표현에는 소유대명사, 전치사 of와 apostrophe s('s)가 있다.
소유대명사는 그 자체로 '~의 것' 이라는 명사의 의미를 지녀 따로 명사를 붙이지 않는다.

    mine   ours   yours his   hers   its   theirs

명사 뒤에 's를 붙여 소유를 나타내기도 한다.
무생물의 소유격은 전치사 of를 써서 표현한다.

01

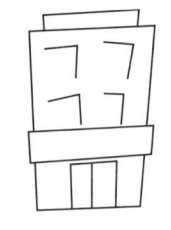

This company is **hers**.

This company is hers. 이 회사는 그녀의 것이다 Is this chair yours? 이 의자는 당신의 것입니까?

02

Is this chair **yours**?

03

The champion is **ours**.

04

That toy is **mine**.

05

This garbage is **his**.

06

This scarf is **hers**.

The champion is ours. 챔피언은 우리의 것이다   That toy is mine. 저 장난감은 내 것이다

This garbage is his. 이 쓰레기는 그의 것이다   This scarf is hers. 이 스카프는 그녀의 것이다

LESSON 14 Possessive Case and "OF" Expressions **73**

07

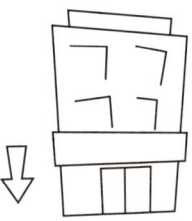

The front **of** the building

08

The roof **of** my house

09

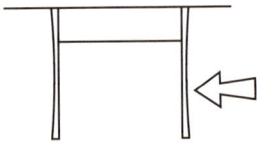

The legs **of** a desk

10

The handle **of** the umbrella

The front of the building 빌딩 앞   The roof of my house 우리 집 지붕

The legs of a desk 책상 다리   The handle of the umbrella 우산 손잡이

11

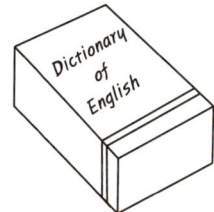

A dictionary **of** English

Must have known!

A dictionary of English 영어 사전   The ladies' shoes 여자 신발

12

The **ladies'** shoes

#1   주체가 무생물일 때도 상황에 따라 's로 소유를 나타낼 수 있다.

#2   s로 끝나는 단어의 경우 발음상 편의를 위해 '만 쓰거나 of로 바꿔준다.

#3   of로 쓰인 소유격의 표현은 of 뒤 부터 해석을 한다.

LESSON 14 Possessive Case and "OF" Expressions

LESSON 15
Wh - Questions wh – 의문문

Wh- 의문문은
의문사 how / what / when / where / which / who / whom / whose / why로 시작되는 의문문이다.

의문사가 항상 문장의 처음에 위치해야 한다.

01

Who is that person?

Who is that person? 저 사람은 누구입니까?
When did you date her? 언제 그녀랑 데이트했어?

02

When did you date her?

03

Where is my cell phone?

Where is my cell phone? 내 핸드폰 어디 있어?   How much is this book? 이 책은 얼마입니까?

04

How much is this book?

05

What time did you get up?

What time did you get up? 아침에 몇 시에 일어났어요?   When did you go to the hospital? 병원에 언제 갔습니까?

06

When did you go to the hospital?

LESSON 15 Wh - Questions **77**

07

Who did you see at the park?

09

How many days are there in a week?

How many days are there in a week? 한 주는 며칠인가요? What are you wearing on your head? 네 머리 위에 무엇을 쓰고 있니?

Who did you see at the park? 공원에서 누구를 보았니? Where is your hometown? 당신의 고향은 어디입니까?

08

Where is your hometown?

10

What are you wearing on your head?

11

When will the stars appear?

Must have known!

When will the stars appear? 별이 언제 뜰까요?   Where is the nearest subway station? 가장 가까운 지하철 역이 어디인가요?

12

Where is the nearest subway station?

#1   wh- + 동사 + 주어?

#2   wh- / how + 조동사 + 주어 + 동사원형?

#3   how + 형용사 / 부사 + be동사 + 주어…?

#4   wh- 의문문은 yes / no로 대답하지 않는다.

LESSON 16
A lot of / a few 수량형용사

A lot of와 a few는 뒤에 오는 명사의 수나 양을 나타내는 수량형용사이다.

A lot of는 '많은', a few는 '조금의' 라는 뜻이다.

01

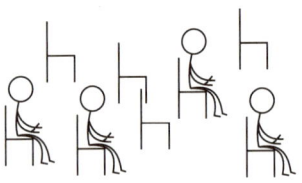

A few of the seats were empty.

A few of the seats were empty. 몇몇 좌석들은 비어 있었다 A lot of people were waiting on the line. 많은 사람들이 줄을 서서 기다리고 있었다

02

A lot of people were waiting on the line.

03

A few of my hat
are on the desk

04

A lot of ants eat cake.

05

They only had **a few** kinds
of food.

06

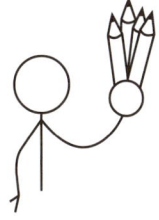

The boy has **a lot of** pencils.

A few of my hat are on the desk 책상 위의 내 모자 몇 개   A lot of ants eat cake. 많은 개미들이 케이크를 먹는다

They only had a few kinds of food. 그들은 몇 가지 음식만 먹었다   The boy has a lot of pencils. 소년은 연필이 많다.

07

A few grains of rice

08

There are **a lot of** dogs on the street.

09

It's only **a few** minutes before closing time.

10

A lot of cars in the parking lot.

A few grains of rice 쌀알 몇 개   There are a lot of dogs on the street. 거리 위에 개들이 많다

It's only a few minutes before closing time. 마감 전까지 몇 분 남지 않았다   A lot of cars in the parking lot. 주차장에 많은 차들

11

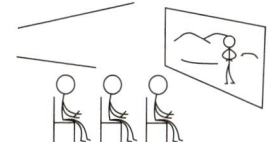

A few people were watching movie.
몇몇 사람들이 영화를 보고 있었다 A woman has a lot of cosmetics. 여자는 화장품을 많이 가지고 있다

12

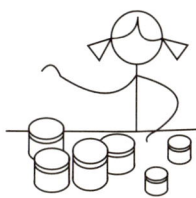

A few people were watching a movie.

Must have known!

A woman has a lot of cosmetics.

#1   A lot of는 부정문, 의문문에서는 잘 쓰이지 않는다.

#2   A few는 셀 수 있는 명사 앞에 붙이는데, 관사가 없이 쓰이는 few에 비해 긍정의 의미를 갖는다.

#3   a lot of = lots of

#4   a lot은 부사 이기 때문에 수량형용사로 나타낼 때엔 반드시 a lot 'of'로 나타내어야 한다.

LESSON 17
Singular and Plural Nouns
단수와 복수

셀 수 있는 명사라면, 단수형과 복수형을 가진다.

복수형이 규칙 변화하는 경우 대부분 명사 뒤에 -s나 -es를 붙이지만, 불규칙하게 변하는 명사는 각각 다르다.

01

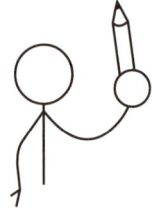

The boy has a **pencil**.

The boy has a pencil. 소년이 연필을 가지고 있다 The boy has a dozen pencils. 소년이 연필 한 다스를 가지고 있다

02

The boy has a dozen **pencils**.

03

Snow White has an **apple**.

Snow White has an apple. 백설공주가 사과를 가지고 있다 Snow White has two apples. 백설공주가 사과 두 개를 가지고 있다

04

Snow White has two **apples**.

05

The **child** has a dirty face.

The child has a dirty face. 아이의 얼굴이 더럽다 The children each have a dirty face. 아이들의 얼굴이 더럽다

06

The **children** each have a dirty face.

07

The **man** is walking on the street.

The man is walking on the street. 남자가 거리를 걷고 있다 The men are walking on the street. 남자들이 거리 위를 걷고 있다

08

The **men** are walking on the street.

09

The boy is a **student**.

The boy is a student. 그 소년은 학생이다
They are students. 그들은 학생이다

10

They are **students**.

11

The guy has a credit card. 그 남자는 신용카드를 가지고 있다 The guy has five credit cards. 그 남자는 신용카드 다섯 개를 가지고 있다

12

The guy has a credit card.

Must have known!

The guy has five credit cards.

#1 -s, -o, -sh, -ch, -x로 끝나는 명사는 보통 -es를 붙여 복수형을 만든다.

#2 -f, -fe로 끝나는 명사는 보통 -ves로 바꾸어 복수형을 만든다.

#3 모음 + y로 끝나는 명사는 그대로 -s를 붙여 복수형을 만든다.

#4 셀 수 있는 명사는 수를 나타내는 형용사 (many, several, few)로 수식 가능하며 앞에 수사를 붙일 수 있다.

LESSON 18
Future – To be going to
미래를 나타내는 be going to

문장에 be going to 의 표현이 있다면 미래를 나타낸다고 보면 된다.

'~할 것이다'로 해석할 수 있는데, 이미 예정되어 있는 일에 쓴다.

01

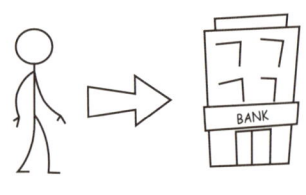

The guy **is going to** go to the bank.

The guy is going to go to the bank. 그 남자는 은행에 갈 것이다 He is going to watch TV. 그는 TV를 볼 것이다

02

He **is going to** watch TV.

03

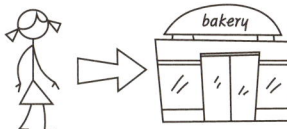

The girl **is going to** go to the bakery.

04

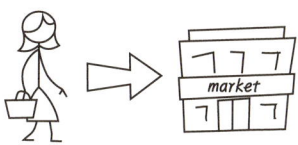

My mom **is going to** go to the market.

05

Cinderella **is going to** run away at 12 o'clock.

06

The turtle **is going to** catch the rabbit.

07

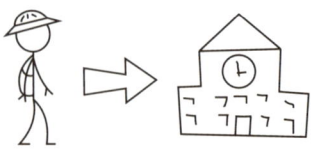

The boy **is going to** go to the school.

09

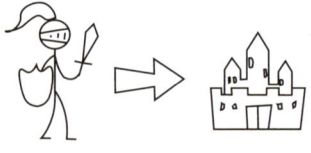

A knight **is going to** go to the castle.

A knight is going to go to the castle. 기사가 성으로 갈 것이다   A woman is going to cook dinner. 여자는 저녁 식사를 준비할 것이다

The boy is going to go to the school. 그 소년은 학교에 갈 것이다   The woodmans is going to drop his ax. 나무꾼이 도끼를 떨어뜨릴 것이다

08

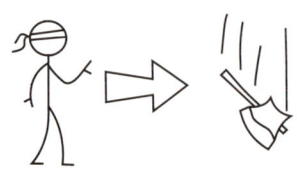

The woodmans **is going to** drop his ax.

10

A woman **is going to** cook dinner.

11

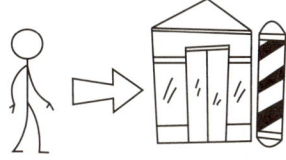

The guy **is going to** cut his hair.

The guy is going to cut his hair. 그 남자는 머리를 깎을 것이다 That car is going to cost 100won. 그 차는 100원 일 것이다

12

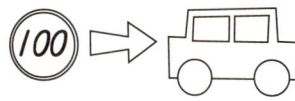

That car **is going to** cost 100won.

Must have known!

#1 am / is / are going to + 동사원형

#2 be going to의 go는 흔히 쓰이는 '가다'의 의미가 아니니 혼동하지 않도록 주의하자.

#3 be going to에서의 to는 전치사가 아닌 to부정사 용법으로 쓰였기 때문에 뒤에 명사가 오게 되면 '가다'의 의미로 쓰이게 되니 유의해야 한다.

LESSON 19
Future – Will 미래

Will 역시 미래를 표현할 때 사용이 가능하다.

도와준다는 뜻의 한자 '助(조)'자가 붙은 조동사의 일종이다.

01

He **will** eat a hamburger in a second.

He will eat a hamburger in a second.
그는 몇 초 안에 햄버거를 먹을 것이다 He will be a great artist. 그는 훌륭한 예술가가 될 것이다

02

He **will** be a great artist.

03

She **will** have a dinner with a guy.

She will have a dinner with a guy. 그녀는 남자와 함께 저녁을 먹을 것이다 The boy will go to bed at 9 o'clock. 소년은 9시에 자러 갈 것이다

04

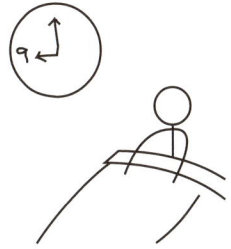

The boy **will** go to bed at 9 o'clock.

05

The woodmans **will** get a golden ax.

The woodmans will get a golden ax. 나무꾼은 금도끼를 받을 것이다 The cookie will disappear soon. 쿠키는 곧 사라질 것이다

06

The cookie **will** disappear soon.

07

He **will** open his magic book.

08

The boy **will** hide under the desk.

09

A girl **will** buy a dress.

10

The bus **will** leave pretty soon.

He will open his magic book. 그는 그의 마법 책을 펼 것이다   The boy will hide under the desk. 소년은 책상 아래 숨을 것이다

A girl will buy a dress. 소녀는 드레스를 살 것이다   The bus will leave pretty soon. 버스는 곧 떠날 것이다

11

The policeman **will** catch the thief.

Must have known!

The policeman will catch the thief.
그 경찰관은 도둑을 잡을 것이다 The cook will cook for himself. 요리사는 자신을 위해 요리할 것이다

12

The cook **will** cook for himself.

#1 will + 동사원형

#2 미래에 대한 의지, 의도에는 be going to를 쓰지 않고 will을 쓴다.

#3 be going to는 will 보다 더 확실하게 예정된 일에 쓰인다.

LESSON 20
Adjectives – Comparison
형용사의 비교급

요즘 '엄친아'라는 말을 흔히 듣는다.
'엄마 친구 아들'이 나보다 더 키가 크고, 더 잘생겼으며, 성적도 더 좋단다. 영어에서는 비교급을 통해 엄친아를 표현해 볼 수 있다.
둘 이상의 대상을 비교할 때는 우리가 배웠던 형용사에 –er을 덧붙여 '더 ~한' 을 나타낼 수 있다 긴 음절의 단어일 경우 앞에 more를 써 처리한다. 셋 이상의 대상 중에 최고의 것은 '최상급' 표현으로 표현해 준다 형용사에 –est를 덧붙여 '제일 ~한'을 나타낼 수 있으며, 긴 음절의 단어는 most를 형용사 앞에 붙여 준다.

01
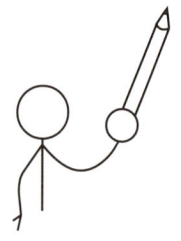

The boy has
the long**est** pencil.

The boy has the longest pencil. 그 소년은 가장 긴 연필을 가지고 있다   The most expensive rock is a diamond. 가장 비싼 돌은 다이아몬드이다

02

The most expensive rock is
a diamond.

03

A boy is bigg**er** than a girl.

A boy is bigger than a girl. 소년이 소녀보다 크다   The turtle was slower than the rabbit. 그 거북은 토끼보다 느렸다

04

The turtle was slow**er** than the rabbit.

05

Seoul Tower is short**er** than the 63building.

Seoul Tower is shorter than the 63building. 서울타워는 63빌딩보다 낮다   A medium pizza is smaller than a large pizza. 미디엄 피자는 라지 피자보다 작다

06

A medium pizza is small**er** than a large pizza.

LESSON 20 Adjectives – Comparison **97**

07

He is **less** fat than he was.

09

More than 5 people

More than 5 people 다섯 명 이상의 사람들
The apple tree is taller than the pine tree. 그 사과나무가 소나무보다 크다

He is less fat than he was. 그는 예전보다 덜 뚱뚱하다   KTX is the fastest train in Korea. KTX는 한국에서 가장 빠른 기차이다

08

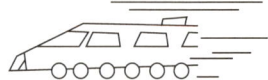

KTX is **the** fast**est** train in Korea.

10

The apple tree is tall**er** than the pine tree.

11

A limousine is long**er** than a regular car.

Must have known!

A limousine is longer than a regular car. 리무진은 보통 차보다 길다   Asia is the biggest continent. 아시아는 가장 큰 대륙이다

12

Asia is **the** bigg**est** continent.

#1 -er 또는 more를 통해 비교할 때는 뒤에 반드시 than이 따라 와야 한다.

#2 최상급의 표현을 쓸 때에는 항상 앞에 the를 붙여 준다.

#3 단어의 길이가 3음절 이상일땐 more를, 미만일때 -er

#4 단모음 + 자음 → 끝의자음 한번 더 쓰고 -er, 자음 + y → y를 i 로 고치고 -er

#5 afraid, asleep, alive, alone 등 a로 시작되는 대부분의 형용사 들은 음절 수 상관없이 more을 쓴다.

다음 이미지를 보고 우측에서 적절한 답에 표시하세요.

01

A It was rainy yesterday.
B It was foggy yesterday.
C It was sunny yesterday.
D It was cloudy yesterday.

02

A We were at the restaurant.
B We were at the department store.
C We were at the swimming pool.
D We were at the bus stop.

03

A The king was a beggar when he was young.
B The king has four brothers.
C The king was younger than the queen.
D The king is still alive.

04

A He is taking a nap.
B She was skating at the square.
C She was walking to the station.
D He is talking on the phone.

05

A The policeman was eating a doughnut.
B The fireman was a can of coke.
C The professor has reading a book.
D The chef was riding a bicycle.

06

A The baby was crying.
B The girl was jumping.
C The people were singing.
D The man was walking.

07

A I have two sisters.
B The boy has a laptop.
C The woman has a diamond ring.
D The girl has a pet.

08

A I had a pencil and a pen in my pocket.
B The boy had two dogs and two cats in his house.
C The girl came home and went to bed.
D The girl had cake and coffee for dessert.

09

A I need to feed my dog.
B Cats have sharp claws.
C There are many animals in the zoo.
D Chickens can't fly high.

10

- A Where is my wallet?
- B Did you bring your books?
- C Is this chair yours?
- D Who are you?

11

- A This scarf is hers.
- B He ate my muffins.
- C Don't throw garbage in here.
- D We can't find you.

12

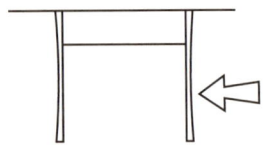

- A This table is made of wood.
- B The legs of a desk
- C The top of a building
- D This chair is broken.

13

- **A** What time is it now?
- **B** Where are you?
- **C** Who is she?
- **D** Where is my cell phone?

14

- **A** What do you want to eat?
- **B** Who did you see at the park?
- **C** Where is my brother?
- **D** Which one is yours?

15

- **A** Where is the nearest subway station?
- **B** When did you come back?
- **C** Where is the bus stop?
- **D** Who is her sister?

16

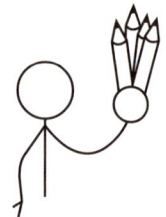

- **A** The boy surprised her.
- **B** I have a lot of books.
- **C** She is pointing at him.
- **D** The boy has a lot of pencils.

17

- **A** A few grains of rice
- **B** A cup of coffee
- **C** Two rabbits
- **D** A bottle of wine

18

- **A** A lot of dogs in the ground
- **B** A lot of cars in the parking lot
- **C** A lot of trucks on the road
- **D** A lot of fish in the river

19

A The girl has a big thumb.
B The woman has a long neck.
C The boy has a dozen of pencils.
D The man has a beard

20

A The girl has blue eyes.
B The boy has long fingers.
C The baby has small feet.
D The child has a dirty face.

21

A The guy has a credit card.
B The man has two cars.
C The girl has a ring.
D The woman has three bags.

22

A She is going to go on a trip.

B We are going to work together.

C He is going to watch TV.

D I am going to throw the ball.

23

A The elephant is bigger than the tiger.

B The turtle is going to catch the rabbit.

C He is taller than her.

D This flower is smaller than that one.

24

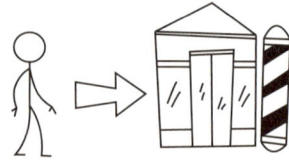

A The guy is going to cut his hair.

B The boy is walking on the street.

C The girl is going to tell her mother.

D We are talking on the phone.

25

- A He has a nice camera.
- B He will be a great artist.
- C He will not attend this class.
- D He is rich.

26

- A A boy will go to a market.
- B A girl will leave this town.
- C A boy will go hiking.
- D A girl will buy a dress.

27

- A The father will give his son some money.
- B The mother will make some cookies for her daughter.
- C The policeman will catch the thief.
- D The boy will finish the homework.

28

A   Seoul Tower is shorter than 63building.

B   The school is smaller than the hospital.

C   The cake is bigger than the cookie.

D   The girl is weaker than the boy.

29

A   Less than 4 people

B   More than 5 people

C   More than 6 people

D   Less than 3 people

30

A   A snake is longer than an earthworm.

B   A giraffe is taller than a camel.

C   A tiger is bigger than a rabbit.

D   A limousine is longer than a regular car.

EXERCISE ACTIVITY ANSWERS

01	C	16	D
02	D	17	A
03	A	18	B
04	B	19	C
05	A	20	D
06	C	21	A
07	C	22	C
08	D	23	B
09	B	24	A
10	C	25	B
11	A	26	D
12	B	27	C
13	D	28	A
14	B	29	B
15	A	30	D

나의 정답 개수

/30

정답 개수가 **24**개 이상이라면
➔ 이제 다음 레슨을 공부하세요

정답 개수가 **24**개 이하라면
➔ 레슨 11로 돌아가서 복습하세요

LESSON 21
Tag Questions 부가 의문문

상대방의 확인, 동의를 구하기 위해 문장의 끝에 짧게 달라붙는 '부가 의문문'이라는 것이 있다.
앞의 문장이 긍정이라면 부가 의문문은 '~그렇지 않니?'의 의미로 부정의 형태를 띠고, 부정이라면 부가 의문문은 '~그렇지?'의 의미로 긍정의 형태를 띤다.
이때, 앞의 문장과 동사가 일치해야 한다.
be동사가 쓰였으면 부가 의문문도 be동사로, do동사가 쓰였으면 부가 의문문도 do 동사로 쓰는 식이다.

01

They are your cups, **aren't they?**

They are your cups, aren't they? 그것들은 너의 컵이지? He is walking to the door, isn't he? 그는 문으로 걸어가고 있지?

02

He is walking to the door, **isn't he?**

03

She is combing her hair,
isn't she?

04

She is combing her hair, isn't she?
그녀는 머리를 빗고 있지, 그렇지? The boy isn't sleeping now, is he? 소년은 지금 깨어 있지, 그렇지?

The boy isn't sleeping now,
is he?

05

The baby stopped crying,
didn't he?

The baby stopped crying, didn't he?
아기는 울음을 그쳤어, 그렇지? That old man can't run very fast, can he? 저 노인은 빨리 못 뛰어, 그렇지?

06

That old man can't run very
fast, **can he?**

LESSON 21 Tag Questions

07

He will be the President,
won't he?

He will be the President, won't he? 그는 대통령이 될 거야, 그렇지? You are still sleepy, aren't you? 너는 아직 졸리지?

08

You are still sleepy,
aren't you?

09

He can't speak English,
can he?

He can't speak English, can he? 그는 영어를 못하지, 그렇지? Students should study hard, shouldn't they? 학생들은 열심히 공부해야 해, 그렇지 않아?

10

Students should study hard,
shouldn't they?

11

You were at the party, weren't you?
너는 파티에 갔지, 그렇지?　There is a tree on the hill, isn't there? 그 언덕에는 나무가 있어, 그렇지?

12

You were at the party,
weren't you?

Must have known!

There is a tree on the hill,
isn't there?

#1　부가 의문문의 주어는 항상 대명사이고, 항상 동사와 합쳐져 '축약형'으로 쓰인다.

#2　앞문장과 뒷문장 동사 간의 시제를 반드시 일치시켜야 한다.

#3　앞문장의 동사가 be동사, 조동사일때 not을 붙이고, 일반동사일 경우에는 do로 바꾸어 부가 의문문을 만든다.

LESSON 22
Interrogative Verb Forms 동사 의문형

어떤 동사를 쓰느냐에 따라 의문문의 구성 요소도 달라진다.

먹다, 마시다, 자다 등 일상적으로 쓰이는 '일반동사'로 의문문을 만들고 싶다면, do 동사의 도움을 받아야 한다. 과거는 did, 현재는 do를 쓰고, do 동사 뒤의 일반동사는 항상 원형으로 쓴다.
what, when, how 등의 의문사가 올 경우 항상 앞에 위치한다.

01

Do you speak English?

Do you speak English? 영어를 할 줄 아세요? Did you do your homework yesterday? 어제 숙제 했니?

02

Did you do your homework yesterday?

03

Does your mother go shopping on Saturdays?

Does your mother go shopping on Saturdays? 너희 어머니는 토요일마다 장 보러 가시니?   Did you bring an umbrella today? 오늘 우산 가져 왔니?

04

Did you bring an umbrella today?

05

Don't you understand the question?

Don't you understand the question? 그 문제가 이해 안 되니?   Are you tired today? 오늘 피곤하니?

06

Are you tired today?

LESSON 22 Interrogative Verb Forms

07

Is your cell phone expensive?

09

Can you carry the box?

Can you carry the box? 상자를 옮겨 줄래요?   What did the boy throw at the dog? 그 소년은 개한테 뭘 던졌니?

Is your cell phone expensive? 네 휴대폰 비싸니?   Does your teacher play the piano? 너희 선생님은 피아노를 치시니?

08

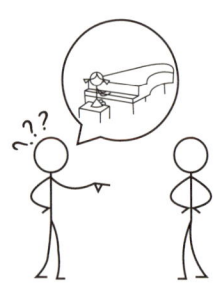

Does your teacher play the piano?

10

What did the boy throw at the dog?

11

Where do you eat lunch?

Must have known!

Where do you eat lunch? 점심을 어디서 먹니? Who is the lady looking for? 숙녀분은 누구를 찾고 있나요?

12

Who is the lady looking for?

#1 be동사/ Do / Does / Did + 동사원형 + 주어…?

#2 wh- / how로 시작하는 의문문
의문사가 주어일 경우 : 〈의문사 + 동사…?〉
의문사가 주어가 아닐 경우 :
〈의문사 + be동사 + 주어…?〉
〈의문사 + 조동사 + 주어 + 동사원형…?〉

LESSON 23
Adverbs 부사

ad + verb
부사는 동사를 꾸며 주는 품사이다.
물론 부사, 형용사를 꾸며 주기도 한다.
부사는 대부분 '형용사 + ly'의 형태이고 '~하게'로 해석한다.

01

People walk slow**ly** on the icy road.

People walk slowly on the icy road. 사람들은 빙판길에서 천천히 걷는다 She carefully laid her baby on the bed. 그녀는 아기를 침대에 조심스럽게 눕혔다

02

She careful**ly** laid her baby on the bed.

03

The thief quiet**ly** ran away from the house.

05

The baby cried loud**ly**.

The baby cried loudly. 아기가 크게 울었다
The gentleman gladly helped the lady.
신사는 기쁜 마음으로 숙녀를 도왔다

The thief quietly ran away from the house. 도둑은 조용히 집에서 도망쳤다   The policeman quickly caught the thief.
경찰관은 재빨리 도둑을 잡았다

04

The policeman quick**ly** caught the thief.

06

The gentleman glad**ly** helped the lady.

LESSON 23 Adverbs

07

The teacher scolded the student angri**ly**.

09

The patient screamed mad**ly**.

The patient screamed madly. 환자는 미친 듯 소리쳤다 The cook divided the cake equally. 요리사는 케이크를 똑같이 나누었다

The teacher scolded the student angrily. 선생님은 화난 듯 학생을 야단쳤다
The princess was beautifully dressed. 공주는 아름답게 옷을 입고 있었다

08

The princess was beautiful**ly** dressed.

10

The cook divided the cake equal**ly**.

11

He left the place hasti**ly**.

Must have known!

He left the place hastily. 그는 급하게 그 장소를 떠났다 The student silently came in the classroom. 학생은 조용히 교실에 들어왔다

12

The student silent**ly** came in the classroom.

#1   부사는 의미를 덧붙이는 역할을 하기 때문에 생략이 가능하다.

#2   일반적으로 부사는 조동사 / be동사 뒤, 일반동사 앞에 위치한다.

#3   그러나 lately, badly, hardly의 경우처럼 모든 형용사 + ly가 부사가 되는 것은 아니다.

LESSON 24
Conjunctions 접속사

접속사는 두 개 이상의 단어, 혹은 문장 사이에 다리를 놓아주는 품사이다.

and는 우리말의 '그리고', or은 '또는', but은 '그러나'에 해당한다.

이 세 가지는 연결하려는 두 개 이상의 대상이 대등한 중요성을 지닐 때 주로 쓰인다.

01

Can we order 2 cups of coffee **and** 2 cups of tea?

Can we order 2 cups of coffee and 2 cups of tea? 커피 두 잔과 차 두 잔을 주실래요? Do you like soup or salad? 수프로 하실래요 아니면 샐러드로 하실래요?

02

Do you like soup **or** salad?

124 ENGLISH GRAPHICS GRAMMAR

03

Put the book on the desk
and the bag on the chair.

05

Take off your coat
and have a seat.

Take off your coat and have a seat. 코트를 벗고 자리에 앉아라   That boy can play the piano and the violin. 소년은 피아노와 바이올린을 칠 수 있다

Put the book on the desk and the bag on the chair. 책은 책상 위에 놓고 가방은 의자 위에 놓아라   You can choose two cell phones or one computer. 너는 휴대폰 2개나 컴퓨터 한 대를 고를 수 있다

04

You can choose two cell
phones **or** one computer.

06

That boy can play the piano
and the violin.

LESSON 24 Conjunctions

07

He can take a taxi
or drive a car himself.

09

You can have the red book
or the yellow book but not
the blue book.

You can have the red book or the yellow book but not the blue book. 빨간 책 이나 노란 책은 가져도 되지만 파란 책은 안 된다   You can take the red pen or the blue pen but not both. 빨간 펜 이나 파란 펜은 가져가도 되지만 둘 다는 안돼.

126 ENGLISH GRAPHICS GRAMMAR

He can take a taxi or drive a car himself. 그는 택시를 타거나 직접 차를 운전할 수 있다   You can have the red book and the yellow book but not the blue book. 빨간 책과 노란 책은 가져도 되지만 파란 책은 안 된다

08

You can have the red book
and the yellow book but not
the blue book.

10

You can take the red pen
or the blue pen but not both.

11

You can go to the beach **and** the swimming pool but not to the mountain.

Must have known!

You can go to the beach and the swimming pool but not to the mountain. 바닷가와 수영장에는 가도 되지만 산은 안돼   You can go to the beach or the swimming pool but not to the mountain. 바닷가나 수영장에는 가도 되지만 산은 안돼

12

You can go to the beach **or** the swimming pool but not to the mountain.

#1 접속사로 연결된 문장들은 반드시 시제가 일치되어야 한다.

#2 접속사의 수 = 동사의 수 – 1

#3 접속사를 두고 중복되는 말이 있을 경우 한쪽에서 생략이 가능하다.

LESSON 25
Expletives 허사

뭣도 없지만 있는 척, 허세를 부리는 사람들이 종종 있다.
영어에 있어서는 expletive가 그런 존재이다.

문장의 주체로 뜻을 가진 것도 아니면서! 주어자리에 위치한다.
There, it, here이 있다.
거기, 이것, 여기로 해석하지 말고, 깔끔히 무시해주자.

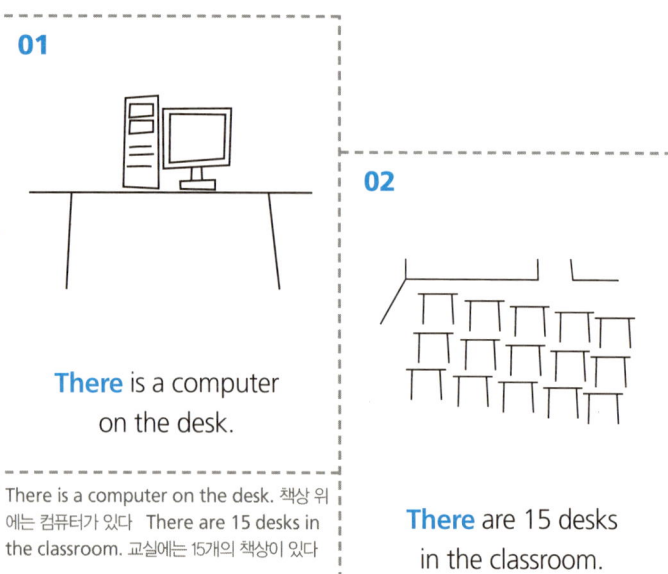

01

There is a computer on the desk.

There is a computer on the desk. 책상 위에는 컴퓨터가 있다   There are 15 desks in the classroom. 교실에는 15개의 책상이 있다

02

There are 15 desks in the classroom.

03

There are many books on the table.

05

Once upon a time, **there** was a king in the country.

Once upon a time, there was a king in the country. 옛날에 왕국에는 왕이 있었습니다   There were 5 chairs in the room. 방 안에 의자가 5개 있습니다.

There are many books on the table. 탁자 위에는 책이 많다   There's not a phone in the office. 사무실에는 전화가 없다

04

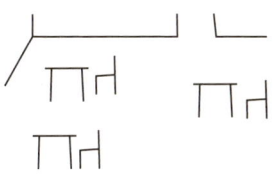

There's not a phone in the office.

06

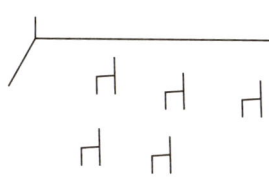

There were 5 chairs in the room.

LESSON 25 Expletives

07

There is nobody in the house.

08

Is **there** a picture in the office?

There is nobody in the house. 집에는 아무도 없다 Is there a picture in the office? 사무실에 그림이 있니?

09

Is **there** anyone in the room?

10

Are **there** many people in the classroom?

Is there anyone in the room? 방에 아무도 없어요? Are there many people in the classroom? 교실에 사람이 많니?

11

There is something behind me, isn't **there**?

Must have known!

There is something behind me, isn't there? 내 뒤에 무언가 있지, 그렇지? There are many people in the stadium, aren't there? 경기장에 사람이 많지, 그렇지?

12

There are many people in the stadium, aren't **there**?

#1 it은 비인칭주어 / 가주어 라고도 표현한다.

#2 비인칭주어 : 날씨, 계절, 시간, 날짜 등을 나타낼때.

#3 가주어 : 주어가 'to 부정사 that절' 일 때 이가 너무 길어질 경우 진짜 주어를 대신하여 쓴다.

LESSON 26
Prepositions of Time 시간을 나타내는 전치사

시간을 나타내는 전치사는 수두룩하게 있다.
대표적인 at, in, on before, after, within, until에 대해 익혀두면 시간에 관한 표현은 무리 없이 해낼 수 있다.
at, in, on은 모두 '~에'라는 뜻을 가지지만 시간의 범위에 따라 쓰임새에는 차이가 있다.
at은 짧게 '시각'을 나타낼 때 쓴다 in은 at보다는 긴 범주의 시간, 이를테면 월, 연도와 함께 쓰인다. on은 좀 더 구체적인 시간 표현과 함께한다. 정해진 날짜나 요일, 특정한 날의 아침, 점심, 저녁을 지칭할 때 쓰인다.

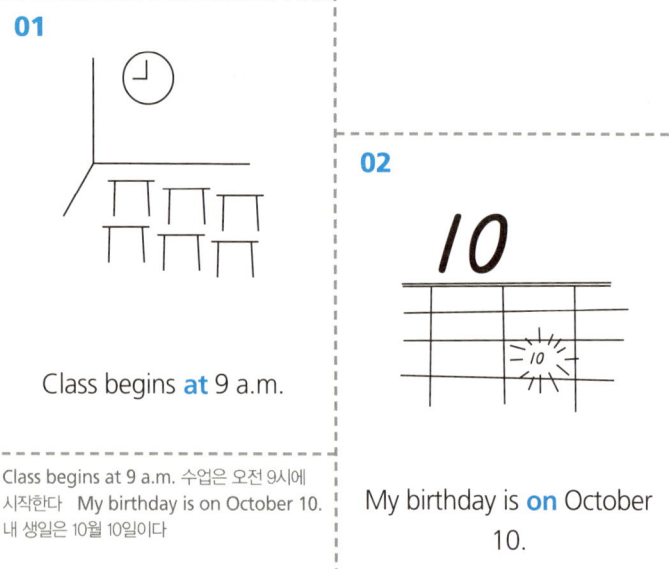

01

Class begins **at** 9 a.m.

Class begins at 9 a.m. 수업은 오전 9시에 시작한다 My birthday is on October 10. 내 생일은 10월 10일이다

02

My birthday is **on** October 10.

03

I have a date **on** Saturday.

I have a date on Saturday. 나는 토요일에 데이트가 있다   He has an appointment at noon. 그는 정오에 약속이 있다

04

He has an appointment **at** noon.

05

The doctor will visit my house **at** 4 o'clock.

The doctor will visit my house at 4 o'clock. 의사는 4시에 우리집을 방문할 것이다
My father usually goes climbing on the weekend. 우리 아버지는 보통 주말에 등산을 가신다

06

My father usually goes climbing **on** the weekend.

LESSON 26 Prepositions of Time **133**

07

That lazy man always gets up late **in** the morning.

That lazy man always gets up late in the morning. 그 게으른 사람은 항상 아침에 늦게 일어난다   The sun rises early in June. 6월에는 해가 일찍 뜬다

08

The sun rises early **in** June.

09

You should finish your homework **before** Tuesday.

10

The package will arrive **after** Monday.

You should finish your homework before Tuesday. 너는 화요일 전에 숙제를 끝내야 한다   The package will arrive after Monday. 소포는 월요일 후에 도착할 것입니다

11

The carpenter will do his job **for** 2 days.

Must have known!

The carpenter will do his job for 2 days. 목수는 2일 동안 일을 할 것이다 The plane will leave in 3 hours. 비행기는 3시간 안에 출발할 것이다

12

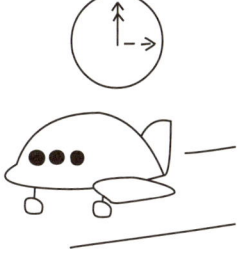

The plane will leave **in** 3 hours.

#1   before는 '～전에', after는 '～후에'의 뜻을 가진다.

#2   within은 일정한 기간 이내에 일어나는 일을 표현할 때 쓴다.

#3   until은 어느 시점까지의 동작이 계속됨을 표현할 때 사용한다.

#4   for은 구체적인 시간과 함께, during은 정확한 시간의 길이가 나타나지 않은 기간을 표현할 때 쓴다.

LESSON 27
Prepositions of Place 장소를 나타내는 전치사

백문이불여일견. 다음의 간단한 그림을 통해
장소를 나타내는 전치사를 익혀보자.

01

The speaker stood **before** the audience.

The speaker stood before the audience. 연사는 청중 앞에 섰다   The computer is on the table. 컴퓨터는 탁자 위에 있다

02

The computer is **on** the table.

03

The chair is **next to** the desk.

05

The fat guy is sitting **beside** the pretty girl.

The fat guy is sitting beside the pretty girl. 뚱뚱한 남자는 예쁜 소녀 옆에 앉아있다
The handsome boy took a seat behind the girl. 잘생긴 소년은 소녀 뒤에 앉았다

The chair is next to the desk. 의자는 책상 옆에 있다 The small boy is standing between the tall guys. 작은 소년은 큰 남자들 사이에 서있다

04

The small boy is standing **between** the tall guys.

06

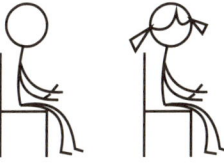

The handsome boy took a seat **behind** the girl.

LESSON 27 Prepositions of Place

07

The tree is **in front of** the building.

08

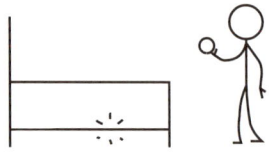

The boy found the money **under** the bed.

09

The pickpocket is standing **in back of** the tourist.

10

The house is **on top of** the hill.

The tree is in front of the building. 나무는 건물 앞에 있다 The boy found the money under the bed. 소년은 침대 밑에서 돈을 찾았다

The pickpocket is standing in back of the tourist. 소매치기는 관광객 뒤에 서있다
The house is on top of the hill. 집은 언덕 위에 있다

11

The cloud flies high **above** the sky.

Must have known!

The cloud flies high above the sky.
구름은 하늘 위로 높이 날아간다 The train passed through the tunnel. 기차는 터널을 통해 지나갔다

12

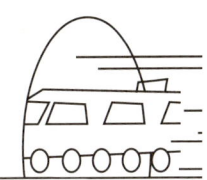

The train passed **through** the tunnel.

#1 전치사는 다른 단어와의 관계를 나타나는 말이다.

#2 전치사 다음에 오는 말은 반드시 목적격이어야 하며 이는 명사, 동명사, 대명사, 간접의문문 등이 있다.

LESSON 28
Abstract Nouns 추상명사

보통 우리가 이해하기 어려운 난해한 그림들은 '추상화'인 경우가 많다.
추상명사도 딱히 꼬집어 말할 수는 없는 난해한 개념들을 지칭한다.

삶과 죽음, 사랑과 증오 등이 추상명사에 포함된다.

01

Children need the **love** of their parents.

Children need the love of their parents.
아이들은 부모의 사랑이 필요하다   The US National Flag is a symbol of democracy.
미국 국기는 민주주의의 상징이다

02

The US National Flag is a symbol of **democracy**.

03

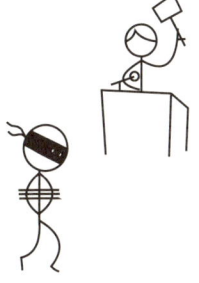

The murderer was finally brought to **justice**.

04

Remove your **hatred** and **love** your enemy.

05

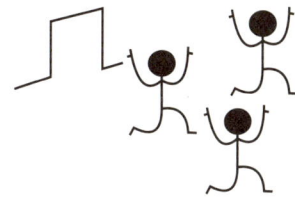

The slaves finally won their **liberty**.

06

Equality between men and women is so important.

The murderer was finally brought to justice. 살인자는 결국 정의의 심판을 받았다 Remove your hatred and love your enemy. 너의 증오를 없애고 원수를 사랑하라

The slaves finally won their liberty. 노예들은 결국 자유를 얻었다 Equality between men and women is so important. 남녀 간의 평등은 정말 중요하다

LESSON 28 Abstract Nouns

07

Worry made him an old man.

Worry made him an old man. 걱정이 그를 노인으로 만들었다 Even a comedian cannot let his sorrow go away. 코미디언도 그의 슬픔을 물러가게 할 수 없다

08

Even a comedian cannot let his **sorrow** go away.

09

Life without her means nothing to him.

Life without her means nothing to him. 그녀가 없는 삶은 그에게 아무 의미도 없다
The boy's lie caused his mom's anger. 소년의 거짓말이 엄마를 화나게 했다

10

The boy's lie caused his mom's **anger**.

11

Happiness doubles when it is shared by all.

Happiness doubles when it is shared by all. 행복은 모두와 공유할 때 배가된다   His father's death was really shocking to him. 그의 아버지의 죽음은 그에게 정말 충격이었다

12

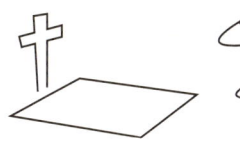

His father's **death** was really shocking to him.

Must have known!

#1   추상명사에는 복수형으로 쓰일 수 없고 부정관사를 앞에 붙이지 말아야 한다.

#2   of + 추상명사는 형용사로 표현된다.

#3   추상명사는 the + 형용사의 형태로 나타나기도 한다.

LESSON 29
Present Perfect 현재완료

현재완료라는 이름은 누가 붙였는지 영 딱딱하다.
이 시제는 과거의 어느 시점을 그 시초로 지금엔 어떤지를 나타낼 때 쓴다.

즉, 과거시제는 과거에 반짝 일어났던 일을 나타낼 때 쓰이지만,
현재완료시제는 과거부터 지금까지 영향력을 끼치는 일에만 쓰일 수 있다.

01

Winter **has come**.

Winter has come. 겨울이 왔다   The student has studied English for 10 years. 학생은 영어를 10년 동안 공부해왔다

02

The student **has studied** English for 10 years.

03

That careless boy **has dropped** his cell phone.

04

Have we **met** before?

05

I **have seen** the Grand Canyon.

06

That guy **has worked** for the company for 12 years.

That careless boy has dropped his cell phone. 저 부주의한 소년은 휴대폰을 떨어뜨렸다   Have we met before? 우리가 만난 적 있나요?

I have seen the Grand Canyon. 나는 그랜드 캐년을 본 적이 있다   That guy has worked for the company for 12 years. 저 남자는 12년 동안 회사를 위해 일해왔다

07

This window **has been broken** for a long time.

This window has been broken for a long time. 이 유리창은 오랫동안 깨져있었다
The movie has moved so many people. 영화는 아주 많은 사람들을 감동시켰다

08

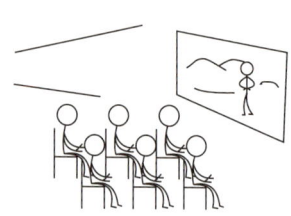

The movie **has moved** so many people.

09

What **have** I **done**?

What have I done? 내가 도대체 무슨 일을 한 거지? Where the heck have you been? 도대체 어디에 있었어?

10

Where the heck **have** you **been**?

11

I have lived in Seoul for 10 years.

I have lived in Seoul for 10 years. 나는 10년 동안 서울에 살아왔다 I haven't been to Korea in 20 years. 나는 20년 동안 한국에 가본 적이 없다

12

I haven't been to Korea in 20 years.

Must have known!

#1   have / has + p.p (과거분사)

#1   여기서 have는 '가지다'라는 뜻이 아닌 단순한 기능적인 의미일 뿐이다.

#1   현재완료는 계속, 결과, 경험, 완료의 4가지 용법을 지닌다.

#1   현재완료의 의문문 〈Have (Has) + 주어 + 과거분사…?〉 이에 대한 답변도 have / has로 한다.

LESSON 29 Present Perfect

LESSON 30
Past Perfect 과거완료

과거완료를 편하게 이해하기 위해서는 타임라인이 도우미가 될 수 있다.

　　　　　대과거　　과거　　현재

과거완료는 현재완료를 한 타임씩 뒤로 옮겨놓은 형태이다.
현재완료가 현재와 과거 사이를 이야기한다면,
과거완료는 과거의 한 시점과 그보다 더 예전의 시점 사이의 일을 이야기 하는데 쓰인다.

01

Galileo **had studied** about the universe before Newton did.

Galileo had studied about the universe before Newton did. 갈릴레이는 뉴튼 이전에 우주를 연구했다 He had already been there when I arrived. 내가 도착했을 때 그는 이미 거기에 있었다

02

He **had** already **been** there when I arrived.

03

My mom **had prepared** dinner for when I came home.

04

The boy said he **had broken** the window.

05

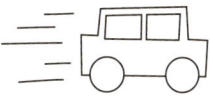

We **had driven** for 2 hours until we got to the place.

06

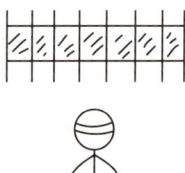

It **had taken** a week for the boy to finish his paper.

My mom had prepared dinner for when I came home. 내가 집에 왔을 때 엄마는 저녁을 준비해놓고 계셨다 The boy said he had broken the window. 소년은 자기가 유리창을 깼다고 말했다

We had driven for 2 hours until we got to the place. 우리는 그 장소에 도착할 때까지 2시간 동안 차를 탔다 It had taken a week for the boy to finish his paper. 소년이 리포트를 끝낼 때까지 1주일이 걸렸다

LESSON 30 Past Perfect **149**

07

The girl **had finished** the test before the boy started it.

The girl had finished the test before the boy started it. 소녀는 소년이 시작하기 전에 시험을 끝냈다   The kidnapper had held the boy until we found him. 유괴범은 우리가 찾을 때까지 소년을 데리고 있었다

08

The kidnapper **had held** the boy until we found him.

09

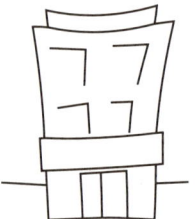

The businessman **had had** the building until he sold it.

The businessman had had the building until he sold it. 사업가는 팔 때까지 건물을 가지고 있었다   Had the guide been there before you arrived? 안내원은 네가 도착하기 전에 거기에 있었니?

10

Had the guide **been** there before you arrived?

150 ENGLISH GRAPHICS GRAMMAR

11

Had you **read** the book before you wrote about it?

Must have known!

Had you read the book before you wrote about it? 감상문을 쓰기 전에 그 책을 읽었어?   Had the gentleman been there before the lady arrived? 신사는 숙녀가 도착하기 전에 거기에 와있었니?

12

Had the gentleman **been** there before the lady arrived?

#1   had + p.p (과거분사)

#2   과거완료는 대과거 라고 부르기도 한다. 어떤 과거의 시점이 다른 과거와 비교 했을 때 더 과거일때를 나타내기 때문이다.

#3   과거 완료가 before이나 after과 함께 쓰이게 되면 단순과거로 표현해도 된다.

#4   과거완료의 의문문 〈Had + 주어 + p.p…?〉
이에 대한 대답도 had로 한다.

LESSON 30 Past Perfect

다음 이미지를 보고 우측에서 적절한 답에 표시하세요.

01

A   He is talking to her, isn't he?

B   You are coming to our house, aren't you?

C   She is combing her hair, isn't she?

D   They are going on a trip, aren't they?

02

A   He can't play the guitar, can he?

B   That old man can't run very fast, can he?

C   You can't understand the question, can you?

D   We are not foreigners, are we?

03

A   Students should study hard, shouldn't they?

B   We should leave now, shouldn't we?

C   He should give it to them, shouldn't he?

D   You should tell me the truth, shouldn't you?

04

- **A** Do you know where the subway station is?
- **B** Do you speak English?
- **C** Does he know about them?
- **D** Do I know you?

05

- **A** Did they invite her?
- **B** Did he go to school?
- **C** Did you bring an umbrella today?
- **D** Did she give you a call?

06

- **A** What did we do yesterday?
- **B** What did the woman bring?
- **C** What did the man say?
- **D** What did the boy throw at the dog?

07

A The baby cried loudly.
B The girl spoke quietly.
C The man walked slowly.
D The woman drove carefully.

08

A The student studied hard.
B The patient screamed madly.
C The boy ate slowly.
D The girl stood quietly.

09

A She walked to him quickly.
B I got up early.
C He left the place hastily.
D She cried sadly.

10

- A Do you like soup or salad?
- B Do you know me?
- C Does he have a sister?
- D Do they know each other?

11

- A Meet him and ask for a help.
- B Take off your coat and have a seat.
- C Go straight and turn right.
- D Close the door and turn on the lights.

12

- A You should go to the hospital and see a doctor.
- B I will go home and take a nap.
- C You can eat spaghetti or a piece of pizza.
- D He can take a taxi or drive a car himself.

13

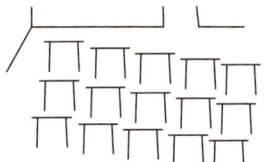

A There are 5 cats in the house.
B There are many books in the library.
C There are 15 desks in the class room.
D There is a dog under the couch.

14

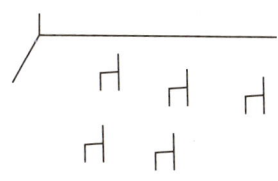

A There were 5 chairs in the room.
B There were 4 desks in the room.
C There were 2 cars in the parking lot.
D There were 3 students in the class room.

15

A Is there a telephone in the building?
B Is there a muffin in the oven?
C Is there a picture in the office?
D Is there an apple in the refrigerator?

16

A He has an appointment at noon.

B The class will start at 9 o' clock.

C I have a meeting at 2 o' clock.

D The lunchtime will start at noon.

17

A The festival starts in April.

B The summer begins in July.

C The school starts in March.

D The sun rises early in June.

18

A The exam will be held for 3 days.

B The carpenter will do his job for 2 days.

C He will stay in Paris for 5 days.

D The rain will continue for 4 days.

19

A The computer is on the table.
B The flower is on the desk.
C The cat is on the table.
D The carpet is on the floor.

20

A The old man stood behind the woman.
B The young boy walked behind the girl.
C The handsome boy took a seat behind the girl.
D The dog sat behind the man.

21

A The kite flies high above the roof.
B The airplane flies high above the cloud.
C The balloon flies high above the sky.
D The cloud flies high above the sky.

22

A Children need the love of their parents.

B The students need their help.

C Our family needs a new car.

D Our class needs a new computer.

23

A They will go to the museum.

B The slaves finally won their liberty.

C The children are playing tennis.

D The parents got angry.

24

A I would like to have an orange juice, please.

B My father looks younger than my brother.

C The boy's lie caused his mom's anger.

D Why don't you come with us?

25

A Summer has come.
B Winter has come.
C Fall has come.
D Spring has come.

26

A I have seen the Grand Canyon.
B Where is my sister?
C You need to calm down.
D Have we met before?

27

A I have been to New York.
B I have eaten too much.
C I have lived in Seoul for 10 years.
D I have no idea.

28

A Last week I had worked for 3 days.

B We had driven for 2 hours until we got to the place.

C The schedule had been delayed 2 hours by a heavy storm.

D I'm glad to have met him.

29

A I had intended to write a letter, but I couldn't.

B The train had already left when we arrived at the station.

C The flowers had been given to her by him on her birthday.

D The girl had finished the test before the boy started it.

30

A Had you read the book before you wrote about it?

B Had we finished just in time?

C Had you finished your homework before you went out?

D Had he met her before we left?

EXERCISE ACTIVITY ANSWERS

01	C	16	A
02	B	17	D
03	A	18	B
04	B	19	A
05	C	20	C
06	D	21	D
07	A	22	A
08	B	23	B
09	C	24	C
10	A	25	B
11	B	26	A
12	D	27	C
13	C	28	B
14	A	29	D
15	C	30	A

나의 정답 개수

/30

정답 개수가 **24**개 이상이라면
→ 이제 다음 레슨을 공부하세요

정답 개수가 **24**개 이하라면
→ 레슨 21로 돌아가서 복습하세요

LESSON 31
Active / Passive Voice 능동태와 수동태

하나의 사실을 전달하기 위해 다양한 방법이 동원될 수 있다.
능동태와 수동태가 그 방법들 중 일부이다.

주어가 행위를 할 수 있는 능력을 지녔다면, 그 문장은 능동태이고,
그렇지 않다면 수동태이다.

01

The boy **drew** a picture on the black board.

The boy drew a picture on the black board. 소년은 칠판에 그림을 그렸다 The girl hit the boy on the head. 소녀는 소년의 머리를 때렸다

02

The girl **hit** the boy on the head.

03

The student **dropped** his pencil.

The student dropped his pencil. 학생은 연필을 떨어뜨렸다   That bald man designed the dress. 저 대머리의 남자가 그 옷을 디자인했다

04

That bald man **designed** the dress.

05

My mother **bought** the shoes.

My mother bought the shoes. 어머니가 신발을 사셨다   My parents play tennis in the morning. 부모님은 아침에 테니스를 치신다

06

My parents **play** tennis in the morning.

LESSON 31 Active / Passive Voice

07

Who **broke** the vase?

08

The ball was **thrown by** the boy.

09

The desk will **be fixed by** the teacher.

10

The clothes **were bought by** my boyfriend.

Who broke the vase? 누가 꽃병을 깨뜨렸지? The ball was thrown by the boy. 공은 소년이 던졌다

The desk will be fixed by the teacher. 책상은 선생님이 고칠 것이다 The clothes were bought by my boyfriend. 옷은 남자친구가 샀졌다

11

That picture **was drawn by** the kid.

That picture was drawn by the kid.
저 그림은 아이가 그렸다   This job will be done by experts. 이 일은 전문가들이 할 것이다

12

This job will **be done by** experts.

Must have known!

#1 수동태 : 주격으로 쓰인 목적격 + be + 과거분사 + by + 목적격으로 쓰인 주격

#2 수동태의 일반적인 의문문 형태 〈be + 주어 + 과거분사…?〉

#3 과거분사가 be동사와 함께 쓰일 경우 be + p.p의 형태로 나타내므로 수동태와 혼동하기 쉽기 때문에 주의해야 한다.

#4 수동의 의미를 갖고 있는 자동사들 (open, read, sell, cut 등)은 수동태의 형태로 바꾸지 않는다.

LESSON 32
Adjective Clause 형용사구

구는 두 개 이상의 낱말이 모여 만들어진 것인데, 절과 달리
주어와 동사를 갖추지 못한 단어 덩어리이다.

형용사구는 형용사에 상당하는 역할을 하고, 명사나 대명사를 꾸며준다.
특히 동사 + ing + 목적어의 형태는 진행의 의미를 가진다.

01

The carpenter is **making** the furniture.

The carpenter is making the furniture.
목수는 가구를 만들고 있다   The ship is
sailing across the ocean. 배는 대양을 향해
하고 있다

02

The ship is **sailing** across the ocean.

168 ENGLISH GRAPHICS GRAMMAR

03

The grandmother was **smiling** at the baby.

The grandmother was smiling at the baby. 할머니는 아기에게 미소 짓고 있었다
The professor was talking about politics. 교수는 정치에 관해 말하고 있었다

04

The professor was **talking** about politics.

05

That fat girl is **working** out very hard.

That fat girl is working out very hard. 저 뚱뚱한 소녀는 매우 열심히 운동하고 있다 The man was walking to the door rapidly. 남자는 문 쪽으로 빠르게 걷고 있었다

06

The man was **walking** to the door rapidly.

LESSON 32 Adjective Clause

07

The Internet is **replacing** TV these days.

08

The travelers were **waving** their hands to us.

09

The meeting is **being** held now.

10

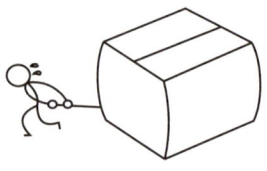

Is the small boy **trying** to move the heavy box?

The Internet is replacing TV these days. 요즘에는 인터넷이 TV를 대체하고 있다 The travelers were waving their hands to us. 관광객들은 우리에게 손을 흔들고 있었다

The meeting is being held now. 회의는 지금 열리고 있다 Is the small boy trying to move the heavy box? 작은 소년은 무거운 상자를 옮기려고 애쓰고 있니?

11

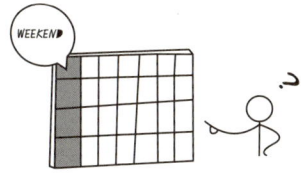

What were you **doing** on the weekend?

Must have known!

What were you doing on the weekend? 주말에 무엇을 하고 있었니?
What is the author writing about? 작가는 무엇에 관해 쓰고 있니?

12

What is the author **writing** about?

#1 형용사구는 보어로 쓰이거나, 진행의 의미를 나타낼 때 사용된다.

#2 보어로 쓰이는 경우
ex) The machine is out of order. (형용사구: out of order)
This computer is of use. (형용사구: of use)

#3 진행의 의미를 나타내는 경우 : 동사 + ing + 목적어
ex) The boy is throwing a ball. (형용사구: throwing)
A baby is eating an apple. (형용사구: eating)

LESSON 33
Too much / Too many 양이 많은 / 수가 많은

too much와 too many는 적당한 양보다 '너무 많은'의 부정적 뜻을 지닌다.

much는 셀 수 없는 명사에, too many는 셀 수 있는 명사에 쓴다.

01

Too many people gathered together.

Too many people gathered together. 너무 많은 사람들이 함께 모였다   Too many people applied for the job. 너무 많은 사람들이 그 일에 지원했다

02

Too many people applied for the job.

03

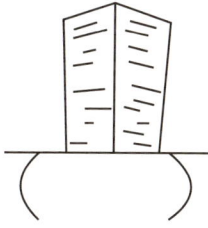

He put **too many** pieces of paper on the table.

04

The tourist should not go to **too many** sites.

05

There are **too many** cars in the parking lot.

06

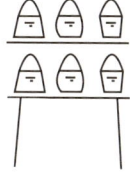 

The woman buys **too many** bags.

07

The newspaper lost **too many** readers.

08

The newspaper lost too many readers. 그 신문은 너무 많은 구독자들을 잃었다   The man smokes too much. 남자는 담배를 너무 많이 피운다

The man smokes **too much**.

09

Too much sugar was used on the food.

Too much sugar was used on the food. 음식에 설탕이 너무 많이 사용되었다   The lady put too much perfume on her clothes. 숙녀는 옷에 향수를 너무 많이 뿌렸다

10

The lady put **too much** perfume on her clothes.

11

There is **too much** furniture in the room.

Must have known!

There is too much furniture in the room. 방에 가구가 너무 많다   She spent too much money on shopping. 그녀는 쇼핑에 너무 많은 돈을 썼다

12

She spent **too much** money on shopping.

#1   too much/too many = more than is good

#2   아무리 ~ 해도 지나치지 않는다 : cannot~ too much

LESSON 34
Future Perfect Progressive
미래완료진행

미래의 어느 시점까지 일정한 기간 동안 동작이 계속되는 것을 의미한다.

문장 내에는 반드시 시간을 나타내는 절 또는 구가 포함된다.
'~ 즈음에는 ~하고 있을 것이다'라고 해석한다.

01

The marchers **will have been walking** for 3 hours at 4 o' clock.

The marchers will have been walking for 3 hours at 4 o'clock. 행진자들은 4시까지 3시간 동안 걷는 것이 된다 The singer will have been singing on the stage tonight. 가수는 오늘밤 무대에서 노래 부르고 있을 것이다

02

The singer **will have been singing** on the stage tonight.

03

In October, the guy **will have been working** out for 5 months.

In October, the guy will have been working out for 5 months. 10월이면 그는 5개월간 운동하는 것이 된다   At 3 o'clock, the woman will have been shopping for 5 hours. 3시면 그녀는 5시간 동안 쇼핑하게 된다

04

At 3 o'clock, the woman **will have been shopping** for 5 hours.

05

The cosmonaut **will have been staying** in space for 1 year next month.

The cosmonaut will have been staying in space for 1 year next month. 다음달이면 우주인은 우주에 1년간 머무르게 된다   Dad will have been sleeping for 3 hours at 5 p.m. 아빠는 5시면 3시간 동안 자는 것이 된다

06

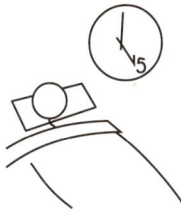

Dad **will have been sleeping** for 3 hours at 5 p.m.

LESSON 34 Future Perfect Progressive

07

Next year, the scientist **will have been working** on the project for 10 years.

Next year, the scientist will have been working on the project for 10 years. 내년이면 과학자는 10년간 그 프로젝트를 연구하게 된다 Will it have been raining for 5 days tomorrow? 내일이면 5일간 비가 오는 것이 되니?

08

Will it **have been raining** for 5 days tomorrow?

09

Will the boy **have been practicing** piano for a week tomorrow?

Will the boy have been practicing piano for a week tomorrow? 내일이면 소년이 피아노를 일주일 동안 연습한 거니? How long will the baby have been crying at 1 o'clock? 한시면 아기가 얼마나 오래 우는 게 되지?

10

How long **will** the baby **have been crying** at 1 o'clock?

11

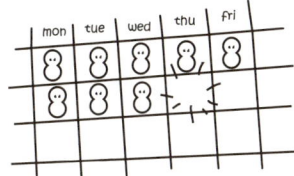

How long **will** it **have been snowing** tomorrow?

Must have known!

How long will it have been snowing tomorrow? 내일이면 얼마나 오래 눈이 오는 것이 되지? How long will the man have been running at noon? 정오면 남자가 얼마나 오래 달리는 것이 되니?

12

How long **will** the man **have been running** at noon?

#1   will / shall + have + been + –ing

#2   미래완료진행은 '~하고 있을 것이다'라고 해석한다.

#3   미래완료진행형에는 수동태를 사용하지 않는다.

LESSON 34 Future Perfect Progressive

LESSON 35
Present Perfect Progressive
현재완료진행

현재 완료 진행형은 앞서 배운 현재 완료와 비슷하다.
현재 완료 시제 중에서도 과거로부터 현재까지 일정기간 동안
계속 진행 중인 동작을 '진행형'으로 쓴다고 생각하면 쉽다.

현재 완료 시제로 쓰였다면 이미 마무리가 지어진 것이지만,
현재 완료 진행형 시제라면 아직도 계속되는 동작이다.

01

The baby **has been crying** for an hour.

The baby has been crying for an hour.
아기가 한 시간 동안 울고 있다 The man has been waiting for the woman for hours. 남자는 여자를 몇 시간 동안 기다려왔다

02

The man **has been waiting** for the woman for hours.

03

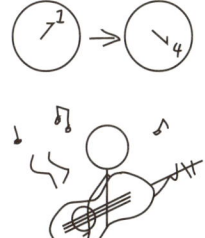

The guy **has been playing** the guitar for 3 hours.

04

They **have been playing** basketball for 2 hours.

05

The guy **has been dancing** since this morning.

06

The man **has been seeing** her since last month.

07

It **has been raining** since 5 o'clock.

It has been raining since 5 o'clock. 5시부터 줄곧 비가 내리고 있다 The couple has been fighting since yesterday. 그 부부는 정오부터 계속 싸우고 있다

08

The couple **has been fighting** since yesterday.

09

The girl **has been looking** at the boy since he came.

The girl has been looking at the boy since he came. 소녀는 소년이 온 후부터 줄곧 그를 보고 있다 Have you been trying to call me since last week? 지난주부터 나에게 전화하려 했니?

10

Have you **been trying** to call me since last week?

11

Has he been walking since this morning? 그는 아침부터 걷고 있니?   Has the student been studying hard for the exam? 학생은 시험공부를 열심히 해왔니?

12

Has he **been walking** since this morning?

Must have known!

Has the student **been studying** hard for the exam?

#1 have / has + been + –ing

#2 현재완료진행은 '~해 오고 있다' 라고 해석한다.

#3 현재완료진행은 상태의 지속으로는 표현하지 않는다.

LESSON 36
Past Perfect Progressive 과거완료진행

과거완료진행형은 훨씬 오래된 과거부터
그 이후의 과거 어느 시점까지 일정한 기간동안 계속된 동작을 나타낸다.

01

The baby **had been crying** when her mom came in.

The baby had been crying when her mom came in. 엄마가 들어왔을 때 아기는 울고 있었다   The mom had been cooking when her son came home. 엄마는 아들이 집에 돌아왔을 때 요리를 하고 계셨다

02

The mom **had been cooking** when her son came home.

03

The girl **had been running** when his friend called him.

05

The guy **had been sleeping** when his boss found him.

The guy had been sleeping when his boss found him. 상사가 그를 찾았을 때 그는 잠을 자고 있었다 They had been eating lunch when they heard the news. 그들은 그 소식을 들었을 때 점심을 먹고 있었다

The girl had been running when his friend called him. 소녀는 그의 친구가 그를 불렀을 때 뛰고 있었다 The boy had been cheating when the teacher saw him. 소년은 선생님이 봤을 때 커닝을 하고 있었다

04

The boy **had been cheating** when the teacher saw him.

06

They **had been eating** lunch when they heard the news.

LESSON 36 Past Perfect Progressive

07

The man **had been drinking** beer when the police arrested him.

08

The woman **had been running** since she had left home.

The man had been drinking beer when the police arrested him. 경찰이 그를 체포했을 때 그는 맥주를 마시고 있었다 The woman had been running since she had left home. 그 여자는 집을 떠난 이래 뛰고 있었다

09

Had the student **been studying** when his dad came in?

Had the student been studying when his dad came in? 학생이 아빠가 들어왔을 때 공부하고 있었니? Had the girl been scratching her head when the doctor saw her? 의사가 봤을 때 소녀는 머리를 긁고 있었니?

10

Had the girl **been scratching** her head when the doctor saw her?

11

Had the soldier been bleeding since he had been shot?

Had the soldier been bleeding since he had been shot? 총을 맞은 이래 병사는 피를 흘리고 있었니? What had the girl been eating when her friends saw her? 소녀는 친구들이 그녀를 보았을 때 무엇을 먹고 있었니?

12

What had the girl been eating when her friends saw her?

Must have known!

#1   had + been + –ing

#2   과거완료진행은 '~했던 중이었다'라고 해석한다.

#3   과거완료진행은 특정하게 한정시킬 수 없는 상황 (시간의 경과, 진행 상황)을 표현한다.

LESSON 37
Future Perfect 미래완료

미래의 어느 일정한 시점까지의 완료, 경험, 결과, 계속을 나타낸다.

미래 시제의 한 종류이므로 어느 정도 '추측'한다는 느낌이 남아있다.

01

The girl **will have studied** for 2 hours at 9 o'clock.

The girl will have studied for 2 hours at 9 o'clock. 소녀는 9시면 2시간 동안 공부하게 된다
That man will have run for an hour at 3 o'clock. 남자는 3시면 1시간 동안 뛰게 된다

02

That man **will have run** for an hour at 3 o'clock.

03

The lady **will have slept** over 5 hours at 6 p.m.

04

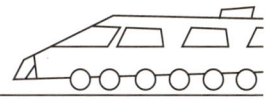

The train **will have arrived** by 7 o'clock.

05

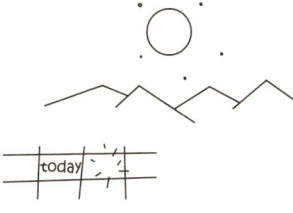

The full moon **will have risen** tomorrow night.

06

The teacher **will have been** in the classroom by then.

The lady will have slept over 5 hours at 6 p.m. 숙녀는 오후 6시면 5시간 넘게 자는 것이 된다   The train will have arrived by 7 o'clock. 기차는 7시까지는 도착해있을 것이다

The full moon will have risen tomorrow night. 보름달이 내일 밤에 떠있을 것이다   The teacher will have been in the classroom by then. 선생님은 그 때까지는 교실에 계실 것이다

07

The boy **will have finished** his homework at 8 p.m.

09

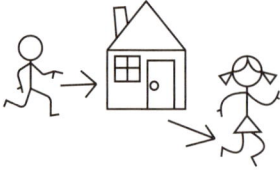

She **will have left** home when her friend comes back.

She will have left home when her friend comes back. 그녀는 친구가 돌아올 때 집을 떠나 있을 것이다 The boy will have cleaned his room before his mother sees it. 소년은 어머니가 보기 전에 자기 방을 치워놓을 것이다

The boy will have finished his homework at 8 p.m. 소년은 오후 8시에 숙제를 끝낼 것이다 The porter will have moved the baggage for 3 hours at 2 o'clock. 짐꾼은 2시면 3시간 동안 짐을 옮긴 것이 된다

08

The porter **will have moved** the baggage for 3 hours at 2 o' clock.

10

The boy **will have cleaned** his room before his mother sees it.

11

Will the guy **have walked** for 3 hours at 4 o'clock?

Must have known!

12

Will the guy have walked for 3 hours at 4 o'clock? 그 남자는 4시면 3시간 동안 걷게 되니? Will you have written your letter for 4 hours at 7 o'clock? 너는 7시면 4시간 동안 편지를 쓰게 된거니?

Will you **have written** your letter for 4 hours at 7 o'clock?

#1 will / shall + have + p.p

#2 미래완료는 미래의 어느 한 시점이 존재하기 때문에 '~하게 되어 있을 것이다' 라고 해석하는 것이 좋다.

#3 미래완료는 미래의 어느시점까지를 표현하기 때문에 'by, until' 이 자주 사용된다.

LESSON 38
Adverbs of Frequency 빈도부사

어떤 일의 빈번한 정도를 나타내주는 부사이다.
문장에 쓰인 동사의 종류에 따라 빈도부사의 위치가 바뀐다.

be동사와 조동사의 뒤에, 일반동사의 앞에 위치한다.
조동사와 일반동사가 같이 있을 경우 빈도부사는 그 사이에 위치한다.

01

The lazy boy **always** gets up late in the morning.

The lazy boy always gets up late in the morning. 그 게으른 소년은 항상 아침에 늦게 일어난다 The mom always tells her children to study hard. 엄마는 항상 아이들에게 열심히 공부하라고 말한다

02

The mom **always** tells her children to study hard.

03

A gentleman is **never** rude to ladies.

05

The professor goes to the museum **often**.

The professor goes to the museum often. 교수는 종종 박물관에 간다   The woman rarely reads this newspaper. 그 여자는 드물게 이 신문을 읽는다

A gentleman is never rude to ladies. 신사는 결코 숙녀에게 무례하지 않는다   That woman usually eats lunch at this restaurant. 저 여자는 보통 이 식당에서 점심을 먹는다

04

That woman **usually** eats lunch at this restaurant.

06

The woman **rarely** reads this newspaper.

LESSON 38 Adverbs of Frequency

07

My friend goes to the theater **very often**.

09

That dog is **always** barking.

That dog is always barking. 저 개는 항상 짖고 있다   The street is always crowded with people. 길은 항상 사람들로 붐빈다

My friend goes to the theater very often. 내 친구는 영화관에 매우 자주 간다
The old man climbs sometimes. 노인은 가끔 등산을 한다

08

The old man climbs **sometimes**.

10

The street is **always** crowded with people.

11

My friend calls me **frequently**.

Must have known!

My friend calls me frequently. 내 친구는 내게 빈번히 전화한다 Do you see movie often? 너는 자주 영화를 보니?

12

Do you see movie **often**?

#1   be동사 + 빈도부사

#2   빈도부사 + 일반동사

#3   조동사 + 빈도부사 + 본동사

LESSON 38 Adverbs of Frequency **195**

LESSON 39
Reflexive Pronouns 재귀대명사

무슨 말이든 반복이 계속되면 지루하기 마련이다.
재귀대명사는 이러한 지루함을 피하기 위해 주로 쓰인다.
한 문장에서 주어와 목적어가 같은 사람인 경우, 또 그것을 강조하고 싶기도 하다면, 재귀대명사가 답이다.

소유격에 -self를 붙이고, 복수일 경우 –selves를 붙인다.
| myself | ourselves | yourself | yourselves |
| him | her | itself | themselves |

01

Please enjoy **yourself**
while you stay here.

Please enjoy yourself while you stay here. 여기 머무시는 동안 마음껏 즐기십시오.
Please help yourself to the dishes. 요리를 마음껏 드십시오.

02

Please help **yourself**
to the dishes.

03

The boy overate all by **himself** on Thanksgiving Day.

05

The woman will pour **herself** a cup of coffee.

The boy overate all by himself on Thanksgiving Day. 소년은 추석에 과식했다
The student overslept all by herself this morning. 학생은 오늘 아침 늦잠을 잤다

04

The student overslept all by **herself** this morning.

06

The magician can touch **himself** on the back easily.

The woman will pour herself a cup of coffee. 여자는 커피를 한 잔 따라 마실 것이다
The magician can touch himself on the back easily. 마술사는 쉽게 등을 만질 수 있다

LESSON 39 Reflexive Pronouns

07

The girl slapped **herself** in the face.

09

The painter drew **himself** on the wall.

The painter drew himself on the wall.
화가는 벽에 자기 자신을 그렸다   He is happy with himself because he has a car. 그는 자동차를 가지고 있기 때문에 행복하다

198 ENGLISH GRAPHICS GRAMMAR

The girl slapped herself in the face.
소녀는 자신의 따귀를 때렸다   The man hits himself on the head when he is wrong.
남자는 그가 틀릴 때에는 자기 머리를 때린다

08

The man hits **himself** on the head when he is wrong.

10

He is happy with **himself** because he has a car.

11

The man is patting **himself** on the back after his success.

Must have known!

The man is patting himself on the back after his success. 그 남자는 성공 후 자기자신을 칭찬하고 있다 The hungry man should get himself some food. 배고픈 남자는 좀 먹어야 한다

12

The hungry man should get **himself** some food.

#1 명령문은 주어가 you이므로 재귀대명사는 yourself 또는 yourselves로 쓴다.

#2 재귀대명사는 강조의 뜻으로 사용되기도 한다.

#3 재귀대명사와 함께 쓰이지 못하는 동사들도 있다는것을 유의해야 한다. (sit down, wake up, relax, remember, complain 등)

#4 장소를 나타내는 전치사에는 재귀대명사를 함께 쓰지 않는다.

LESSON 40
For / Since 시간을 나타내는 전치사

for와 since는 시간과 관계 있는 문장이라면 정말 자주 쓰이는 전치사이다.

for는 시작점과 끝점

for는 '~동안', since는 '~부터' 또는 '~이래'의 뜻이다.

01

The poor guy has been running **for** 3 hours.

The poor guy has been running for 3 hours. 그 불쌍한 남자는 3시간 동안 뛰고 있다
The couple has dated for 5 months. 그 커플은 5개월 동안 사귀어왔다

02

The couple has dated **for** 5 months.

200 ENGLISH GRAPHICS GRAMMAR

03

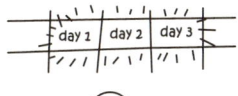

The student read the book **for** 3 days.

The student read the book for 3 days.
학생은 3일 동안 그 책을 읽었다   The girl thought about it for a few minutes.
소녀는 몇 분 동안 그것에 대해 생각했다

04

The girl thought about it **for** a few minutes.

05

The man closed his eyes **for** a few seconds.

The man closed his eyes for a few seconds. 그는 몇 초동안 눈을 감았다   The clerk showed me the product just for a second. 점원은 내게 그 제품을 겨우 잠깐만 보여주었다

06

The clerk showed me the product just **for** a second.

LESSON 40 For / Since

07

The scientist studied about dinosaurs **for** 20 years.

The scientist studied about dinosaurs for 20 years. 과학자는 20년 동안 공룡에 대해 연구했다 In summer, it rains for a very long time. 여름에는 비가 아주 오랫동안 온다

08

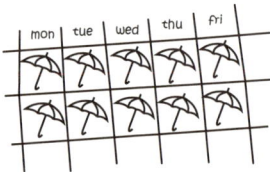

In summer, it rains **for** a very long time.

09

The girl has been watching TV **since** 7 o'clock.

The girl has been watching TV since 7 o'clock. 소녀는 7시부터 TV를 보고 있다 The guy has been sleeping since yesterday. 그 남자는 어제부터 계속 자고 있다

10

The guy has been sleeping **since** yesterday.

11

The woman has been writing a book **since** last week.

Must have known!

The woman has been writing a book since last week. 여자는 지난 주 이래 책을 쓰고 있다 The team has practiced baseball since last month. 그 팀은 지난 달 이래 야구를 연습해왔다

12

The team has practiced baseball **since** last month.

#1   for + 기간 (명확한 숫자의 형태)

#2   since + 특정한 시점

#3   접속사로서의 for, since와 혼동할 수 있으니 주의해야 한다. (이들뒤엔 주어 + 동사 형태가 따라온다)

LESSON 40 For / Since

다음 이미지를 보고 우측에서 적절한 답에 표시하세요.

01

- A The girl threw the ball to the boy.
- B The boy jumped over the girl.
- C The girl hit the boy on the head.
- D The boy hit the girl on the shoulder.

02

- A We watched an ice hockey match.
- B He waited with her for an hour.
- C My mother bought the shoes.
- D My dad bought me a necklace.

03

- A The ball was thrown by the boy.
- B The picture was drawn by the girl.
- C The ceremony was held by our family.
- D The pizza was made by the woman.

04

A The dog is running across the ground.

B The ship is sailing across the ocean.

C The car is rushing through the tunnel.

D The man is running through the gate.

05

A The boy was riding a bicycle.

B The girl was dancing on the floor.

C The woman was walking on the phone.

D The man was walking to the door rapidly.

06

A The travelers were waving their hands to us.

B The babies were crying altogether.

C The man was eating a hamburger.

D The girl was reading a book.

07

A There's only one student left in the classroom.

B Five people are waving their hands.

C Too many people gathered together.

D The kids fell asleep.

08

A There are too many cars in the parking lot.

B There are two dogs in the living room.

C There is no one in the room.

D There is a vase on the table.

09

A He ate too many hamburgers.

B You put too much sugar in here.

C She spent too much money on shopping.

D You spoke too much.

10

A The boy will have been staying in China for a month next week.

B At 3 o' clock, the woman will have been shopping for 5 hours.

C In July, the girl will been studying for 2 months.

D The boy will have been playing soccer for 3 hours tomorrow.

11

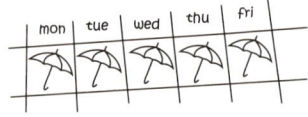

A Will it have been raining for 5 days tomorrow?

B Will he have been practicing violin for 3 hours next Monday?

C Will you have been exercising for 2 hours tomorrow?

D Will it have been snowing for 2 days?

12

A How long will the girl have been taking a nap at noon?

B How long will the woman have been sewing?

C How long will the boy have been driving a motorcycle?

D How long will the man have been running at noon?

13

- A The boy has been waiting for the girl for 3 hours.
- B The baby has been crying for an hour.
- C The woman has been cooking meals for an hour.
- D The man has been reading a book for 2 hours.

14

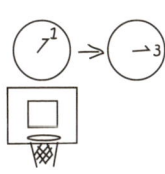

- A They have been playing basketball for 2 hours.
- B I have been driving a car for half an hour.
- C We have been staying here for an hour.
- D They have been singing for 15 minutes.

15

- A It has been snowing since 7 o'clock.
- B It has been sunny since 2 o'clock.
- C It has been raining since 5 o'clock.
- D It has been foggy since 1 o'clock.

16

A The boy had been playing games when the girl arrived.

B The man had been sleeping until the woman woke him up.

C The girl had been studying until the boy sang a song.

D The mom had been cooking when her son came home.

17

A They had been eating lunch when they heard the news.

B They had been cheating until the teacher came.

C They had been doing homework when their parents came home.

D They had been playing tennis when it started to rain.

18

A Had the boy been studying when his mom came home?

B Had the girl been scratching her head when the doctor saw her?

C Had you been eating my lunch when I came in?

D Had the students been playing soccer when the bell rang?

19

A The train will have arrived by 7 o' clock.

B The sky will have been sunny.

C The boy will have studied over 2 hours at 3 p.m.

D The man will have been there at 2 p.m.

20

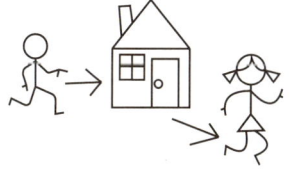

A He will have gone to church when his mom comes back.

B I will have walked to school when you call me.

C She will have left home when her friend comes back.

D You will have met him before she comes back.

21

A Will you have gone shopping for 2 hours at 7 o'clock?

B Will they have moved their luggage when he comes home?

C Will the girl have exercised for an hour at noon?

D Will the guy have walked for 3 hours at 4 o'clock?

22

A She always takes a walk every morning.

B The lazy boy always gets up late in the morning.

C I always go to the gym in the afternoon.

D The old man always reads a newspaper in the morning.

23

A That woman usually eats lunch at this restaurant.

B The young man usually comes at 7 o' clock.

C The policeman usually comes every Sunday.

D The work usually takes 3 hours.

24

A Do you go to an amusement park often?

B Do you visit your hometown often?

C Do you see movies often?

D Do you see her often?

25

A The boy overate all by himself on Thanksgiving Day.

B The girl finished the homework all by herself.

C The woman did an excellent job all by herself.

D The man learned Spanish all by himself.

26

A The boy stepped himself on the foot.

B The girl slapped herself in the face.

C The man touched himself on the shoulder.

D The woman smashed herself in the face.

27

A The old man saw himself in the mirror.

B The boy introduced himself to the class.

C The girl made herself happy.

D The painter drew himself on the wall.

28

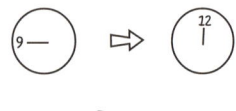

A The boy has been crying for an hour.

B The girl has been eating for 20 minutes.

C The poor guy has been running for 3 hours.

D The woman has been standing for 2 hours.

29

A The man closed his eyes for a few seconds.

B The market is closed for 5 days.

C The exam is held for 3 days.

D The store is opened for 2 days

30

A The exhibition has been held since yesterday.

B The team has practiced baseball since last month.

C The company has started services since last June.

D The man has done his job since last year.

EXERCISE ACTIVITY ANSWERS

01	C	16	D
02	C	17	A
03	A	18	B
04	B	19	A
05	D	20	C
06	A	21	D
07	C	22	B
08	A	23	A
09	C	24	C
10	B	25	A
11	A	26	B
12	D	27	D
13	B	28	C
14	A	29	A
15	C	30	B

나의 정답 개수

/30

정답 개수가 **24**개 이상이라면
→ 이제 다음 레슨을 공부하세요

정답 개수가 **24**개 이하라면
→ 레슨 31로 돌아가서 복습하세요

LESSON 41
Other / Another 부정대명사 the other과 another

other는 '다른'의 뜻을 가지는 형용사이다 절대 혼자 쓰이지 않고 뒤에 명사를 달거나, the를 붙인 형태로 사용해야 한다.

the other는 정해진 개수 내의 대상을 지칭할 때 쓰인다.
여러 개 중 하나, 그리고 그 나머지에서 '그 나머지'에 해당하는 것을 표현할 때 other를 사용하게 되는데, 하나일 경우 the other, 복수일 경우 the others로 표현한다.
another로 지칭할 수 있는 대상은 범위가 제한되어 있지 않다.
'하나 그리고 또 하나'라는 표현에서 '또 하나'에 해당한다.

01

The boy is eating **another** apple.

The boy is eating another apple. 소년은 사과를 하나 더 먹고 있다   The teacher gave us another homework assignment. 선생님은 우리에게 또 다른 숙제를 냈다

02

The teacher gave us **another** homework assignment.

03

The girl will read **another** book after she reads this one.

05

The girl bought **another** cell phone.

The girl bought another cell phone. 소녀는 또 다른 휴대폰을 샀다 The policeman found another wallet on the street. 경찰관은 길에서 또 하나의 지갑을 발견했다

The girl will read another book after she reads this one. 소녀는 하나를 다 읽은 후 책 한 권을 또 읽을 것이다 The father gave another toy to his little son. 아버지는 어린 아들에게 또 하나의 장난감을 주었다

04

The father gave **another** toy to his little son.

06

The policeman found **another** wallet on the street.

LESSON 41 Other / Another **217**

07

The lady is waiting for **another** taxi.

08

His brother will eat **the other** piece of the cake.

09

The guy is reading **the other** book.

10

That boy will use **the other** pencil.

The lady is waiting for another taxi. 숙녀는 또 다른 택시를 기다리고 있다   His brother will eat the other piece of the cake. 그의 동생은 케이크의 다른 한 쪽을 먹을 것이다

The guy is reading the other book. 그는 다른 책을 읽고 있다   That boy will use the other pencil. 저 소년은 다른 연필을 쓸 것이다

11

The mother told her son to do **the other** assignment.

Must have known!

The mother told her son to do the other assignment. 어머니는 아들에게 다른 숙제를 하라고 말했다 The student should read the other books, too. 학생은 나머지 다른 책들도 읽어야 한다

12

The student should read **the other** books, too.

#1   other + 복수명사

#2   another + 단수명사 another - an / other로 생각하면 편하다.

#3   부정대명사는 정해져 있지 않은 대상을 가리킬때 사용한다.

#4   대상이 둘 일 경우 하나 one 나머지 the other

#5   대상이 셋 이상일 경우 처음 one 그 다음의 것 another 나머지 전부 the other(s)

LESSON 42
Adverbs of Time 시간을 나타내는 부사

부사 almost와 still은 시간을 나타낼 때 쓴다.

almost는 '거의', still은 '아직도', '여전히'란 뜻이다.

01

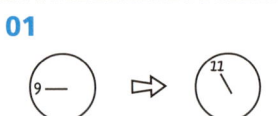

That baby has been crying for **almost** 2 hours.

That baby has been crying for almost 2 hours. 저 아기는 거의 2시간 동안 울고 있다   The children played basketball for almost 5 hours. 아이들은 거의 5시간 동안 야구를 했다

02

The children played basketball for **almost** 5 hours.

220 ENGLISH GRAPHICS GRAMMAR

03

The girl read the book for **almost** 5 days.

The girl read the book for almost 5 days. 소녀는 거의 5일 동안 그 책을 읽었다   The building has been there for almost 30 years. 그 건물은 거의 30년 동안 거기에 있었다

04

The building has been there for **almost** 30 years.

05

He waited for his girl friend for **almost** 9 hours.

He waited for his girl friend for almost 9 hours. 저 남자는 여자친구를 거의 9시간 동안 기다렸다   Students had to study for the test for almost 3 days. 학생들은 거의 3일 동안 시험공부를 해야 했다

06

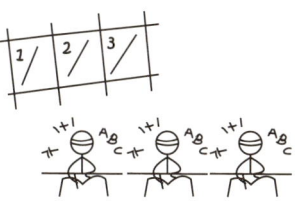

Students had to study for the test for **almost** 3 days.

LESSON 42 Adverbs of Time

07

The poor boy is **still** standing in front of the hallway.

09

My father is **still** a teacher.

My father is still a teacher. 아버지는 아직 선생님이시다   Is your mother still a baker? 너의 어머니는 아직 제빵사이시니?

The poor boy is still standing in front of the hallway. 그 불쌍한 소년은 여전히 복도 앞에 서있다   The Christmas tree is still in the church. 크리스마스 나무는 아직 교회 안에 있다

08

The Christmas tree is **still** in the church.

10

Is your mother **still** a baker?

11

He is **still** working for the construction company.

Must have known!

He is still working for the construction company. 그는 아직 건설 회사에서 일하고 있다 Her boy friend still loves her. 그녀의 남자친구는 여전히 그녀를 사랑한다

12

Her boy friend **still** loves her.

#1   almost + 형용사 / 부사

#2   still + 형용사 / 부사

LESSON 43
Comparison of Adverbs 부사의 비교급

형용사도 비교급으로 쓸 수 있다면, 부사 역시 가능하다.
일부 형용사의 경우 부사로도 쓰일 수 있어 뜻만 빼고는 모든 것이 일치한다.

해석은 상황, 문맥에 따라 해주면 된다.
부사의 비교급, 최상급 만들기는 앞서 배웠던 형용사와 하는 방법이 완전 동일하다.

01

The airplane moves **faster** than the boat.

The airplane moves faster than the boat. 비행기는 배보다 빨리 이동한다 This guy walks quicker than that guy. 이 남자가 저 남자보다 빨리 걷는다

02

This guy walks **quicker** than that guy.

03

He is standing **nearer** to the door than she.

05

The girl runs **the fastest** in her class.

The girl runs the fastest in her class.
그 소녀가 반에서 가장 빨리 뛴다   That lady bought more shoes than my mother.
저 숙녀가 우리 어머니보다 구두를 더 많이 샀다

He is standing nearer to the door than she. 그는 그녀보다 문에 더 가깝게 서있다
That boy walks the quickest in his class.
저 소년이 반에서 가장 빨리 걷는다

04

That boy walks **the quickest** in his class.

06

That lady bought **more** shoes than my mother.

LESSON 43 Comparison of Adverbs **225**

07

This computer works **better** than that one.

08

My car runs **slower** than his.

09

Who earns money the **most**?

10

The lady is dressed **more beautifully** than my wife.

This computer works better than that one. 이 컴퓨터가 저것보다 더 잘 작동한다
My car runs slower than his. 내 차가 그의 것보다 더 느리게 달린다

Who earns money the most? 누가 돈을 가장 많이 버니? The lady is dressed more beautifully than my wife. 그 숙녀가 내 아내보다 더 아름답게 옷을 입고 있다

11

Who walked on the ice the **most carefully**?

Must have known!

Who walked on the ice the most carefully? 누가 가장 조심스럽게 얼음 위를 걸었니? That boy will enter the room the latest. 저 소년이 가장 늦게 방에 들어갈 것이다

12

That boy will enter the room **the latest**.

#1 원급 어미에 -er, -est를 덧붙인다.

#2 3음절 이상의 부사는 원급 앞에 more, most를 놓는다.

#3 원급 비교로 표현할땐 as 부사 as, 해석시엔 뒤의 as만 보고 '~만큼'이라고 해석한다.
ex) Amy is as kind as Tom. → Amy는 Tom만큼 친절하다.

#4 -er, more~로 사용된 표현들은 반드시 than을 빼먹지 말아야 한다.

LESSON 44
Body Parts 신체부위

머리, 어깨, 무릎, 발, 무릎, 발.. 을 영어로 하면?

신체부위의 영어명칭은 한 두 번씩 들어 보았을 법도 하다.
이번 기회에 확실히 다져보자.

01

His **nose** is bleeding.

His nose is bleeding. 그는 코피가 난다
That girl has big eyes. 저 소녀는 눈이 크다

02

That girl has big **eyes**.

03

The boy is touching his **ears**.

05

The ball hit him on the **head**.

The ball hit him on the head. 그 공은 그의 머리를 때렸다   The lady was washing her hands. 숙녀는 손을 씻고 있었다

The boy is touching his ears. 소년은 귀를 만지고 있다   The man opened his mouth widely. 남자는 입을 크게 벌렸다

04

The man opened his **mouth** widely.

06

The lady was washing her **hands**.

LESSON 44 Body Parts

07

I got my **hair** cut.

I got my hair cut. 나는 머리를 깎았다
That man is bending his neck. 저 남자는 목을 구부리고 있다

08

That man is bending his **neck**.

09

The boy is spreading his **legs**.

The boy is spreading his legs. 소년은 다리를 벌리고 있다 The student crossed his arms. 학생은 팔짱을 꼈다

10

The student crossed his **arms**.

230 ENGLISH GRAPHICS GRAMMAR

11

The guy lays on his **back**.

Must have known!

The guy lays on his back. 그는 등을 대고 눕는다   The boy got down on his knees before his mom. 소년은 엄마 앞에 무릎을 꿇고 앉았다

12

The boy got down on his **knees** before his mom.

#1   머리카락은 복수형으로 표현하지 않는다. hairs (x) → hair

#2   tooth의 복수형은 teeth로 나타낸다.

LESSON 45
Count / Non-Count Nouns
셀 수 있는 명사와, 셀 수 없는 명사

셀 수 있는 명사와 셀 수 없는 명사를 구분하는 것은 생각보다 간단하다 물을 컵이나 통처럼 '들이'의 단위로 셀 수 있겠지만, 물 자체를 셀 수는 없다.
이러한 명사를 물질명사라고 하며 셀 수 없는 명사에 들어간다.

이전에 배웠던 사랑과 같은 감정의 추상명사도 셀 수 없는 명사에 포함된다.
이외에 셀 수 있는 명사는, 당장 눈앞의 책상만 봐도 연필, 지우개부터 가방까지, 단어의 뒤에 –s를 덧붙여 복수형을 표현해준다.

01

The boy put some **oranges** on the floor.

The boy put some oranges on the floor. 소년은 오렌지 몇 개를 바닥에 놓았다
My mother bought many grapes tonight. 어머니는 오늘밤 포도를 많이 사셨다

02

My mother bought many **grapes** tonight.

03

There are many **cars** on the street now.

04

That girl really loves **dogs**.

05

The chef put **a fork** on the table.

06

Students read many **books** in school.

There are many cars on the street now. 지금은 거리에 차가 많다   That girl really loves dogs. 저 소녀는 정말 개를 좋아한다

The chef put a fork on the table. 요리사는 식탁에 포크를 하나 놓았다   Students read many books in school. 학생들은 학교에서 많은 책을 읽는다

LESSON 45 Count/Non-Count Nouns

07

In New York, there are so many tall **buildings**.

In New York, there are so many tall buildings. 뉴욕에는 정말 높은 빌딩이 많다
There are so many stars in the sky. 하늘에는 정말 많은 별이 있다

08

There are so many **stars** in the sky.

09

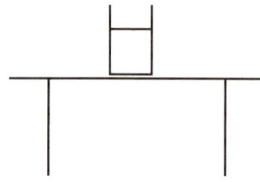

The man put some **sugar** on the table.

The man put some sugar on the table. 그는 약간의 설탕을 식탁 위에 놓았다 The lady drank much water after dinner. 숙녀는 저녁식사 후 물을 많이 마셨다

10

The lady drank much **water** after dinner.

11

The guy needs a lot of **money**.

Must have known!

The guy needs a lot of money. 그는 많은 돈이 필요하다 The woman is drinking a cup of coffee. 그녀는 커피 한 잔을 마시고 있다

12

The woman is drinking a cup of **coffee**.

#1 셀 수 없는 명사에는 -s를 붙이지 않는다.

#2 셀 수 없는 명사의 수량을 나타내려면 앞에 따로 단위명사가 붙는다.
ex) a cup of milk

#3 셀 수 없는 명사 앞에는 a / an을 쓸 수 없다.

LESSON 46
Contractions 축약형

미국인들은 간편한 것을 좋아한다.

이러한 사고방식이 주어와 be동사를 합치기에 이르렀다.
am / are / is의 경우 앞 자를 하나 빼고 주어와 아포스트로피로 연결해준다. (I'm, She's)
will은 wi를 빼고 주어와 아포스트로피로 연결해준다. (He'll)
축약형은 be동사외에 일부 조동사의 부정형에서도 가능하다.
do not을 don't로, can not을 can't로 줄여준다.

01

I'm having dinner right now.

I'm having dinner right now. 나는 지금 저녁을 먹고 있어 He's walking on the street. 그는 길에서 걷고 있다

02

He's walking on the street.

03

She's sleeping on the couch.

05

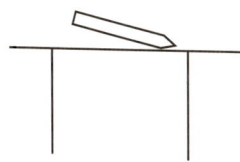

It's on the desk if you need a pencil.

It's on the desk if you need a pencil. 연필이 필요하면 책상 위에 있어   They're running in the gym. 그들은 체육관에서 뛰고 있어.

She's sleeping on the couch. 그녀는 소파에서 자고 있다   You're a good dancer. 춤을 잘 추시는 군요.

04

You're a good dancer.

06

They're running in the gym.

LESSON 46 Contractions   **237**

07

I'll read a book tonight. 나는 오늘밤 책을 읽을 거야 You'll run faster if you exercise hard. 너는 열심히 연습하면 더 빨리 뛰게 될 거야

I'll read a book tonight.

08

You'll run faster if you exercise hard.

09

He'll take a taxi this evening.

He'll take a taxi this evening. 그는 오늘 저녁 택시를 탈 거야 She'll ride a bicycle tomorrow. 그녀는 내일 자전거를 탈 거야

10

She'll ride a bicycle tomorrow.

11

They'll go shopping on Sunday. 그들은 일요일에 쇼핑을 갈 거야   The boy can't swim very well. 소년은 수영을 그다지 잘할 수 없다

12

They'll go shopping on Sunday.

Must have known!

The boy can't swim very well.

#1   will not의 축약형은 won't로 표현한다.

#2   would와 had는 'd로 축약하여 표현한다.

#3   is의 축약형과 소유격을 혼동하기 쉬우므로 주의해야 한다.
ex) he is → he's / his = he's

LESSON 47
Clock Time 시계읽기

바디랭귀지를 떠난 회화를 위해서는 일상에 자주 언급되는 시간에 대해서도 확실히 알아놓아야 한다.

시간을 표현하는 방법은 세가지 정도가 있다.
정시의 경우 숫자 + o' clock의 표현을 써 시간을 나타낼 수 있다. (7 o'clock - 7시)
가운데에 콜론(:)으로 시와 분을 구분하고, a.m.(오전)과 p.m.(오후)를 덧붙여 시간을 표현하기도 한다. (5:30am - 오전 5시 30분)

01

That guy usually gets up at **6 o'clock**.

That guy usually gets up at 6 o'clock. 그 남자는 보통 6시에 일어난다   The boy's class starts at 9 a.m. 소년의 수업은 오전 9시에 시작한다

02

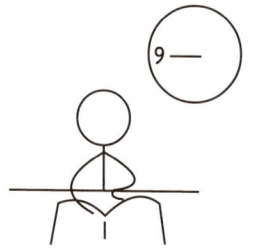

The boy's class starts at **9 a.m.**

03

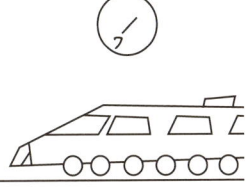

The train will arrive at **7 p.m.**

05

The meeting will begin at **3 o'clock**.

The meeting will begin at 3 o'clock. 회의는 3시에 시작할 것이다   The girl eats breakfast at 7 o'clock in the morning. 소녀는 아침 7시에 아침을 먹는다

The train will arrive at 7 p.m. 기차는 오후 7시에 도착할 것이다   The lady will have dinner at 8 o'clock. 숙녀는 8시에 저녁을 먹을 것이다

04

The lady will have dinner at **8 o'clock**.

06

The girl eats breakfast at **7 o'clock** in the morning.

LESSON 47 Clock Time

07

The soccer game will start at **8:45**.

09

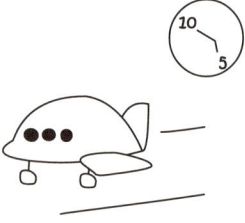

The plane is leaving at **5:50 p.m.**

The plane is leaving at 5:50 p.m. 비행기는 오후 5시50분에 떠난다 The ship will leave at 8:30 in the morning. 배는 아침 8시 반에 떠날 것이다

The soccer game will start at 8:45. 축구는 8시45분에 시작한다 The bus usually arrives here at 9:10 a.m. 버스는 보통 오전 9시10분에 도착한다

08

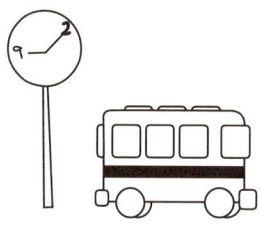

The bus usually arrives here at **9:10 a.m.**

10

The ship will leave at **8:30** in the morning.

11

The baseball team will be there at about **7 o'clock**.

The baseball team will be there at about 7 o'clock. 야구팀은 약 7시경에 거기에 도착할 것이다   The taxi will arrive at the park at around 3:30. 택시는 약 3시 반경에 공원에 도착할 것이다

12

The taxi will arrive at the park at around **3:30**.

Must have known!

#1 30분은 half, 15분은 a quarter로 바꾸어 표현하기도 한다.

#2 to / of를 사용하여 ~전 이라고 표현한다.
ex) a quarter to eight = 8시가 되기 15분전 = 7 : 45

#3 past / after를 사용하여 ~을 지나서 라고 표현한다.
ex) a quarter past three = 3:15

LESSON 48
Do / Does / Did do 동사

do동사는 여러 가지로 활용이 되는 중요한 기본동사이다.
be동사가 주로 상태를 나타내는데 쓰인다면,
do동사는 동작과 관련이 깊다 '~하다'로 해석할 수 있다.

부정문이나 의문문에서 일반동사를 도와주는 조동사로 활약하기도 한다.
현재형은 주어에 따라 1, 2인칭은 do로, 3인칭은 does로 쓰며
과거형은 did, 과거분사형은 done으로 쓴다.
미래는 will + do로 표현이 가능하다.

01

Do you know how to play tennis?

Do you know how to play tennis? 너는 테니스 치는 법을 아니?   Do you take a bus to school? 학교에 갈 때 버스 타니?

02

Do you take a bus to school?

03

Do you have a motorcycle?

05

Do they sell stamps at the store?

Do they sell stamps at the store? 가게에서 우표를 파니? Does the boy go to the movies often? 소년은 영화를 자주 보러 가니?

Do you have a motorcycle? 너 오토바이 있니? Do they play basketball after school? 그들은 학교 끝나고 농구를 하니?

04

Do they play basketball after school?

06

Does the boy go to the movies often?

LESSON 48 Do / Does / Did **245**

07

Does she study in the library after school?

Does she study in the library after school? 그녀는 방과 후에 도서관에서 공부하니? Does the man work for your company? 그는 너의 회사에서 일하니?

08

Does the man work for your company?

09

Does the lady work out in the gym?

Does the lady work out in the gym? 그 숙녀는 체육관에서 운동하니? Does anyone speak English here? 여기서 영어 하는 사람 있어요?

10

Does anyone speak English here?

11

Did you order the pizza?

Must have known!

Did you order the pizza? 네가 피자를 시켰니? Did your father bring the dog? 너의 아버지가 개를 데려왔니?

12

Did your father bring the dog?

#1   do / did + 동사원형 (do동사가 조동사로 쓰일 때)

#2   do동사는 본동사로도 쓰이고 조동사로도 쓰인다.

#3   강조를 하기 위해 do(조동사) + 동사원형 의 형태로 나타낸다.

LESSON 49
Adverb Clauses 부사구

부사구는 두 개 이상의 단어가 모여 형성된 덩어리로 주어와 동사를 갖추지 않는다.

부사구는 동사, 형용사, 또는 문장 전체를 꾸며주는 역할을 한다. 또한 부사구는 문장 내에서 부가적인 역할을 하기 때문에 어떤 형식에서나 쓰일 수 있다.

01

The boy will go skiing **on Saturday**.

The boy will go skiing on Saturday. 소년은 토요일에 스키 타러 갈 것이다   That man always takes a walk in the evening. 저 남자는 항상 저녁에 산책을 한다

02

That man always takes a walk **in the evening**.

03

The lady walks fast **at night**.

04

My father usually hurries up **in the morning**.

05

The guy always takes a nap **in the afternoon**.

06

The mother hugged her daughter **on her birthday**.

The lady walks fast at night. 그 숙녀는 밤에 빨리 걷는다   My father usually hurries up in the morning. 아버지는 아침에 보통 서두르신다

The guy always takes a nap in the afternoon. 남자는 항상 오후에 낮잠을 잔다
The mother hugged her daughter on her birthday. 어머니는 생일날 딸을 안아주었다

07

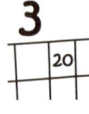

The baseball game will be held
on March 20.

09

The girl will go hiking
in summer.

The girl will go hiking in summer. 소녀는 여름에 하이킹을 갈 것이다 The snowman will melt in spring. 눈사람은 봄에 녹을 것이다

The baseball game will be held on March 20. 야구경기는 3월20일에 열릴 것이다
The singer sang her song on October 7. 가수는 자기 노래를 10월7일에 불렀다

08

The singer sang her song
on October 7.

10

The snowman will melt
in spring.

11

The leaves fall **in fall**.

Must have known!

The leaves fall in fall. 잎은 가을에 떨어진다
That river is frozen in winter. 저 강은 겨울에 언다

12

That river is frozen **in winter**.

#1 부사구는 전치사구의 형태로 나타나거나 to부정사의 부사적 용법으로 쓰인다.

#2 전치사구의 형태로 쓰이는 경우
ex) I will eat dinner at 5 o'clock. (부사구: at 5 o'clock)
She came back on Wednesday. (부사구: on Wednesday)

#3 to부정사의 부사적 용법으로 쓰이는 경우
ex) He studied hard to pass the exam. (부사구: to pass the exam)
We did our homework to play outside. (부사구: to play outside)

LESSON 50
Noun Clause 명사절

주어와 동사를 갖춘 문장이 그보다 더 긴 문장 내에서
주어, 목적어, 보어 자리에 위치해 있을 때,
이 문장을 명사절이라고 지칭한다.

의문사가 명사절을 이끈다.

01

He showed me **what he bought**.

He showed me what he bought. 그는 그가 산 것을 내게 보여주었다 The lady told us where she went shopping. 숙녀는 어디에서 쇼핑했는지 우리에게 말했다

02

The lady told us **where she went shopping**.

03

Nobody knows **who drove the car.**

05

The girl didn't tell the boy **why she hit him.**

The girl didn't tell the boy why she hit him. 소녀는 소년에게 왜 그를 때렸는지 말해주지 않았다 The man doesn't tell me how he can run so fast. 그는 어떻게 그렇게 빨리 달릴 수 있는지 내게 말해주지 않는다

Nobody knows who drove the car. 아무도 차를 운전한 사람을 모른다 The teacher tells us when he will give us homework. 선생님은 언제 우리에게 숙제를 내줄지 말해준다

04

The teacher tells us **when he will give us homework.**

06

The man doesn't tell me **how he can run so fast.**

LESSON 50 Noun Clause **253**

07

The man told the lady **that he loved her**.

The man told the lady that he loved her. 그는 그녀에게 사랑한다고 말했다   What the woman drinks every day is healthy. 그 여자가 매일 마시는 것은 건강에 좋다

08

What the woman drinks every day is healthy.

09

Who hit the boy is difficult to find out.

Who hit the boy is difficult to find out. 누가 소년을 때렸는지는 알아내기 어렵다   When the game will begin is not known yet. 경기가 언제 시작될 지는 아직 알려지지 않았다

10

When the game will begin is not known yet.

11

Where we can find the place is a hard question.

Must have known!

Where we can find the place is a hard question. 어디서 그 장소를 찾을 수 있는가는 어려운 문제이다   Why the girl was scolded by the teacher is a secret. 왜 소녀가 선생님께 혼났는지는 비밀이다

12

Why the girl was scolded by the teacher is a secret.

#1 명사절은 문장 안에서 주어, 동사의 보어, 목적어로 쓰인다.

#2 명사절이 주어로 쓰일 때엔, 문장 내 두 번째 동사 앞에까지를 주어로 본다.

#3 명사절은 '~것' '~하기' 로 해석한다.

#4 명사절은 whether, if, that으로 시작하는 것과 간접의문문으로 시작하는 것이 있다.

다음 이미지를 보고 우측에서 적절한 답에 표시하세요.

01

A   The clerk offered us another shirt.

B   There was another pencil on the table.

C   The boy gave her another notebook.

D   The teacher gave us another homework assignment.

02

A   The old woman gave another apple to the baby.

B   The teacher taught us another way to solve the problem.

C   The father gave another toy to his little son.

D   The kid ate another banana.

03

A   The girl will eat the other piece of the pizza.

B   That boy will use the other pencil.

C   The children will go to the other place.

D   The man will stay for the other night.

04

A The children played basketball for almost 5 hours.

B The girl studied for almost 3 hours.

C The young boy slept for almost 4 hours.

D The children watched TV for almost an hour.

05

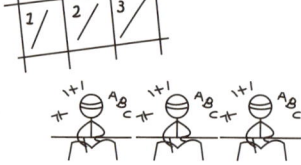

A The girls had to stay in their houses for almost 5 hours.

B The concert had to be prepared for almost 4 days.

C Students had to study for the test for almost 3 days.

D The boy had to wait at the bus stop for almost an hour.

06

A Is your father still a lawyer?

B Is your brother still a student?

C Is your sister still a singer?

D Is your mother still a baker?

07

A The rabbit runs faster than the turtle.

B The airplane moves faster than the boat.

C The kangaroo jumps higher than the frog.

D The helicopter flies higher than the balloon.

08

A That boy walks the quickest in his class.

B That girl runs the fastest in her class.

C That boy jumps the highest in his class.

D That girl swims the fastest in her team.

09

A The girl feeds the dog more carefully than the boy.

B The man is impressed more deeply than the woman.

C This machine works more effectively than that one.

D The lady is dressed more beautifully than my wife.

10

A That girl has big nose.
B That girl has big mouth.
C That girl has big eyes.
D That girl has big ears.

11

A The boy is touching his ears.
B The boy is touching his eyes.
C The boy is touching his hands.
D The boy is touching his nose.

12

A That man is bending his ear.
B That man is bending his neck.
C That man is bending his nose.
D That man is bending his leg.

13

- A My father bought many oranges today.
- B My uncle bought many watermelons tonight.
- C My aunt bought many carrots today.
- D My mother bought many grapes tonight.

14

- A The chef ate a banana on the table.
- B The chef cleaned the table.
- C The chef put a fork on the table.
- D The chef cooked spaghetti.

15

- A There are so many stars in the sky.
- B There are so many balloons in the sky.
- C There are so many airplanes in the sky.
- D There are so many clouds in the sky.

16

- A I'm going to church right now.
- B I'm having dinner right now.
- C I'm reading a book right now.
- D I'm playing computer games right now.

17

- A They're riding bicycles.
- B They're eating cookies.
- C They're playing basketball.
- D They're running in the gym.

18

- A She'll ride a bicycle tomorrow.
- B I'll go home after this class.
- C He'll buy tickets tonight.
- D We'll leave this town tomorrow.

19

A The boy's class starts at 8 a.m.
B The boy's class starts at 3 p.m.
C The boy's class starts at 9 a.m.
D The boy's class starts at noon.

20

A The meeting will begin at 7 o'clock.
B The meeting will begin at 3 o'clock.
C The meeting will begin at 8 o'clock.
D The meeting will begin at 10 o'clock.

21

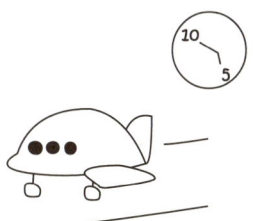

A The plane is leaving at 5:50 p.m.
B The plane is leaving at 3:15 p.m.
C The plane is leaving at 7:20 a.m.
D The plane is leaving at 10:30 a.m.

22

A Do you know how to solve this problem?

B Do you know how to play tennis?

C Do you know how to get to the station?

D Do you know how to eat this food?

23

A Do they know each other?

B Do they have computers in their room?

C Do they play basketball after school?

D Do they go to the gym?

24

A Does anyone speak English here?

B Does anyone have extra paper?

C Does anyone know about her?

D Does anyone listen to the radio?

25

- A That man always takes a walk in the evening.
- B That girl always takes a walk in the morning.
- C That boy always goes to the gym in the evening.
- D That woman always goes to the gym in the morning.

26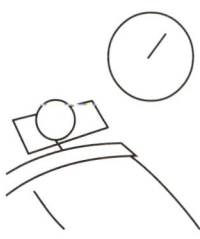

- A I always have an appointment in the afternoon.
- B The young girl always plays tennis in the afternoon.
- C The guy always takes a nap in the afternoon.
- D We always have lunch together in the afternoon.

27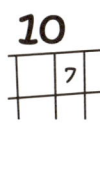

- A The singer sang her song on April 28.
- B The singer sang her song on October 7.
- C The singer sang her song on March 17.
- D The singer sang her song on June 4.

28

A Nobody knows who ate the cake.
B Nobody knows who stole the piano.
C Nobody knows who told him.
D Nobody knows who drove the car.

29

A The man told the lady that he loved her.
B The boy gave her presents that she wanted.
C The woman told him what she saw.
D The girl showed him what she bought.

30

A Who hit the boy is easy to find out.
B Who loved the boy is difficult to find out.
C Who hit the boy is difficult to find out.
D Who told the boy is easy to find out.

EXERCISE ACTIVITY ANSWERS

01	D	16	B
02	C	17	D
03	B	18	A
04	A	19	C
05	C	20	B
06	D	21	A
07	B	22	B
08	A	23	C
09	D	24	A
10	C	25	A
11	A	26	C
12	B	27	B
13	D	28	D
14	C	29	A
15	A	20	C

나의 정답 개수

/30

정답 개수가 **24**개 이상이라면
→ 이제 다음 레슨을 공부하세요

정답 개수가 **24**개 이하라면
→ 레슨 41로 돌아가서 복습하세요

MEMO

MEMO

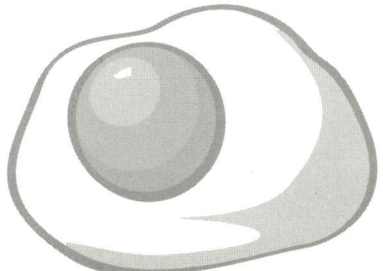

MEMO

MEMO

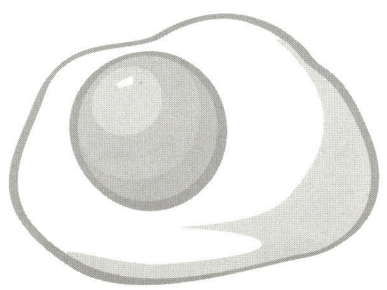

English
Graphics
Grammar